THE MAN WHO CLAIMED TO BE GOD

THE MAN WHO CLAIMED TO BE GOD

DAVID HEWETSON

AN ALBATROSS BOOK

© David Hewetson 1990

Published in Australia and New Zealand by
Albatross Books Pty Ltd
PO Box 320, Sutherland
NSW 2232, Australia
in the United States of America by
Albatross Books
PO Box 131
Claremont, CA 91711, USA
and in the United Kingdom by
Lion Publishing plc
Peter's Way, Sandy Lane West
Littlemore, Oxford OX4 5HG, England

First edition 1990

*This book is copyright. Apart from any fair
dealing for the purposes of private study,
research, criticism or review as permitted
under the Copyright Act, no part of this book
may be reproduced by any process without the
written permission of the publisher.*

National Library of Australia
Cataloguing-in-Publication data

>   Hewetson, David
>   The man who claimed to be God
>
>   ISBN 0 86760 033 0 (Albatross)
>   ISBN 0 7459 1193 5 (Lion)
>
>   1. Jesus Christ. I. Title, II. Title: Jesus
>
>   232'

Cover illustrations: Michael Mucci
Printed by Singapore National Printers

Contents

1 Finding the real Jesus *7*

2 History in the making *18*

3 The Jesus story *28*

4 The kingdom of God *40*

5 Life in the kingdom *51*

6 Claims and miracles *61*

7 The titles of Jesus *73*

8 Death and resurrection *86*

Discussion questions 100

1

Finding the real Jesus

WHO WAS JESUS CHRIST? Was he just a man, though a very great one – perhaps the greatest? Was he a religious genius – the most perceptive spiritual mind that has ever appeared? Was he God's prophet – the long-awaited world king or messiah? Was he actually God in human form?

Jesus himself foresaw that people would ask this question. He once asked his disciples, 'Tell me, who do people say I am?' After receiving their varied answers, he said, 'But who do you say that I am?' In fact, it was only when he was satisfied that the disciples understood the real truth about him that Jesus moved into the most critical phase of his ministry: teaching about his coming suffering and then resolutely making his way to Jerusalem to be executed. Knowing who he is, therefore, is a matter of the utmost importance. To every generation the question comes afresh: 'Who do *you* say that I am?'

Who is Jesus?

The first answers to this question were given by the first Christians. The New Testament as a collection of the earliest writings about Jesus tells us about his character, his teaching, his powers and his claims – as well as describing his life, death and resurrection. Later we will look more closely at some of these themes. But for the moment we can be sure that, as British scholar Donald Guthrie says about the New Testament documents: 'The total impression from a careful study of them leaves no doubt that the Jesus who lived and ministered on earth rapidly became recognised in his risen status as God as well as man.'

The New Testament writers did not attempt to explain such a mystery. They simply reported it, leaving the explanation to others. For them, there was no tension involved in Jesus being the transcendent, pre-existent Son of God and, at the same time, a human being. Perhaps they felt that any attempt to sort out the stupendous miracle called 'Jesus' could only be crude and clumsy, and rob them of its breathtaking wonder. At any rate, the New Testament writers simply accepted Jesus for what he was and rejoiced in knowing him.

The next Christians had, however, a more difficult task. They soon discovered that people were all too prone to overemphasise one aspect of Christ's being and so lose perspective. They soon found they had to try and grapple with the mystery of the incarnation and to formulate statements that would exclude some of these errors.

This is why the Christians of the second and third centuries produced the creeds of the Christian church. As inheritors of their work, we can be grateful that they did this. Just as it is important to be open to the full impact of the New

Testament's testimony to Jesus, so it is necessary to be armed against the restless tendency of the human mind to wander away from the truth that is in Jesus.

Some false ideas about Jesus

In the first centuries it was necessary for Christian teachers to spell out very clearly the fact that Jesus was both true God and true man. They did this as a corrective against the unbalanced teachings of various groups. For example, the Ebionites (second century) concluded that Jesus was a mere man – though an exceptionally holy one – whom God 'adopted' as his Son at his baptism. On the other hand the Docetists (also second century) so emphasised Jesus' divinity that they claimed that he only 'seemed' to be human.

As early theologians grappled with each problem in turn, offering various correctives, the creeds as we know them emerged – honed and perfected to express rather tersely, but very correctly, what was involved in God becoming man. For example, the councils of Nicea (AD 325) and Constantinople (AD 381), reacting against the influential teaching of Arius, produced the Nicene Creed. This clear declaration that the Son is as fully divine as the Father gave us a magnificent weapon against error.

It was essential that answers to these questions should be formulated and agreed upon by the mainstream of Christian thinking. Many departures from the New Testament's presentation of Jesus have leaned to one or other of the two positions mentioned above: Christ's divinity or his humanity. The early Christian creeds have spelled out answers to the more complex questions about who Jesus is, so protecting us against error and distortion.

Many of the modern answers to the question 'Who is Jesus?' would be a lot easier for us to deal with if they were asked within the same framework. The old answers were given by those who, despite their differences, had a strong confidence in the Bible and a firm belief in the supernatural. But many of the new answers are far from that. They have arisen on the other side of a watershed in human thinking.

Scholars and sceptics

The sixteenth, seventeenth and eighteenth centuries in Europe were the cradle of modern thought. In the eighteenth century there arose the intellectual movement called 'the Enlightenment'. In many ways it picked up and developed influences which were already around.

In particular the Enlightenment:

(a) locked into the Renaissance's celebration of the excellence of human beings and the dignity of the mind,

(b) encouraged a supreme trust in the human mind, elevating reason above revelation,

(c) fostered a sceptical and questioning spirit, attacking what the past revered and opposing all traditional authorities,

(d) developed a new critical approach to the Bible that played down the miraculous and supernatural.

Because of its supreme confidence in human reason, this new approach saw miracles as carry-overs from a superstitious past. Miracles did not occur in the new scientific world so, it was argued, they could never have happened even in the days of Jesus and the apostles. Jesus was increasingly seen as a mere man, even if a remarkable one, and thus began 'the quest for the historical Jesus'.

This was an attempt to discover the 'real' Jesus, the simple human figure half-buried beneath the overlay of doctrine with which a credulous church had complicated him and his message. He was still very great – a religious genius, a superlative teacher, a courageous hero, a peerless character – but hardly God's incarnate Son. Many 'lives of Jesus' were written during the nineteenth century but, based on a mutilated Bible, they tended merely to reflect the ideals of the time or of the people who produced them.

It is, of course, a tribute to the greatness of Jesus that people can somehow see in him a mirror for their best and highest hopes; it testifies to the universality of his life and teaching. But it does not allow him 'to be himself'. If we are permitted to read into Jesus what *we* are, he will soon not be the Saviour who reaches down to lift us up so much as an echo-chamber for our best (and less than best) ideals.

Caricature Christs

This process of imposing one's own ideas on Jesus did not cease with the nineteenth century. It still applies to certain approaches to him today. Often influential theologians have imbibed current philosophies and then turned to the New Testament to see whether or not they can find the essence of their ideas in Jesus.

For example, the German theologian Rudolf Bultmann (1884-1976) claimed that supernatural beliefs like the incarnation and resurrection are 'myths' of the outdated, pre-scientific world of the first disciples, framed to express the greatness of Jesus to them. For modern people to accept his message, miracles must be explained away so that the gospel of Christ can be made appropriate to our own time.

The 'political Christ' of the liberation theologians is of much the same kind: he is a revolutionary figure who comes to liberate the poor and the downtrodden, to overthrow oppressive power structures and set people free.

In a more frivolous vein, the alternative culture Jesus of the 1970s – the gentle hippy figure who sends up the establishment and gathers street people to himself, or the enigmatic hero of 'Jesus Christ Superstar' – are lightweight versions of the same process of reading one's own commitments into the New Testament.

No doubt these images of Jesus pick up some insights that have been overlooked by traditional theology. But they impose such a heavy philosophic burden on the New Testament that the authentic Jesus is hidden from sight.

It is ironic that the original 'questers' after the historical Jesus, who accused the church of overlaying him with doctrines, have put on him weights vastly more heavy and less congenial than the ones they tried to remove. They have indeed rolled a huge stone over his door and, if Jesus were not the master of resurrection, we might despair of ever seeing him again! If death could not hold him, neither could these deadening theories. When we abandon such presumptuous ideas and turn to the New Testament with open minds and hearts, he comes to us again as divine, human and alive as ever.

Facing truth honestly

What do we see when we put aside our preconceived notions of Jesus and approach the New Testament at face value, letting it speak for itself? After all, the various sceptical interpretations which have been imposed on Jesus do not form one united picture; they tend more to conflict and cancel each other out.

How, for example, could the gentle Galilean of one interpreter co-exist with the wild revolutionary of another? Or, if we come to the Bible firmly convinced that the miraculous cannot occur and must be stripped away, how could we possibly give these testimonies to Jesus a fair chance? We must come enquiringly, even reverently to the Jesus story and open up our whole personality to its impact. Only then can we formulate a realistic answer to Jesus' age-old question: 'Who do *you* say that I am?'

What sort of Jesus do we find when we let the New Testament speak for itself? Jesus was not a myth, but a man – he was a real, flesh-and-blood human being, located geographically in Palestine at a particular point in history.

❏ He appears as a remarkably balanced person: strong yet tender, shrewd yet believing, active yet prayerful.

❏ He was sympathetic and compassionate, especially towards people burdened with guilt.

❏ He was not afraid to associate with those who were moral and social outcasts.

❏ He appeared to genuinely enjoy being with people and, as his parables show, he was an astute observer of everyday life.

❏ His mind was swift and direct, imaginative and poetic, and he had a keen appreciation of nature and humanity's place in it.

Jesus obviously had about him an air of great personal authority: he could walk untouched through a hostile crowd and he could call disciples to leave all and follow him – and they did. He was totally God-conscious and had a way of inspiring others with his own confidence in God.

Elements in the mosaic
(a) His remarkable character

From any point of view, Jesus was a remarkable person. But we must go further than that. He had a moral purity and an essential goodness that is sometimes described as 'sinlessness'. This is a poor word for our purpose, being a negative term used to describe a positive quality. For Jesus had a kind of moral health or wholeness in which there was no place for evil. He was tempted like other people – no doubt more fiercely than they – but he triumphed over sin and maintained an unbroken fellowship with his Father.

(b) His amazing teaching
It is generally recognised that Jesus has never been surpassed as a teacher of ethics – at least there have been no advances on what he taught in nearly twenty centuries. There is a width, scope and timelessness about his teaching which makes it applicable to all times and all places. Even his enemies were forced on one occasion to admit that 'no man ever spoke like this man'. The power of Jesus' thought, with its wit and insight into human nature, continues to fascinate people today.

(c) His miraculous powers
A third piece of the mosaic needs to be put in place. Jesus had extraordinary powers, especially in the area of healing. Such abilities were not tricks to impress the gullible, but part of his message – a demonstration of the coming of God's kingdom to our world. The scepticism we examined earlier which sought to peel away the supernatural was actually moving further away from the real Jesus. It was trying to remove a vital clue to his identity. His miracles were an essential part of his message! In seeking an answer to the question 'Who is Jesus?' there is certainly no escape from the miraculous.

(d) His astounding claims
With his claims the question of who is Jesus is most sharply focussed. Perhaps the best person in

human history could also be the world's greatest teacher. Perhaps God could also work healing wonders through him. But if he made huge claims for himself, then – unless his *claims* were true – he would completely demolish his credibility.

The fact is that Jesus placed *himself* central to his own teaching. He claimed to be 'one' with God and able to do what God alone could do: judge people, forgive sins, control the forces of nature. Any explanation other than that Jesus was God in human form creates enormous difficulties.

Could one who majored on humility and truth in his teaching perpetuate a lie? How does that fit in with the sheer goodness of his character? And if he was mistaken, what kind of a person must he have been: a psychological misfit? A mad egomaniac playing God? How does that mesh with his obvious wisdom and his penetrating insight into human behaviour?

As C.S. Lewis put it: 'The discrepancy between the depth and sanity and (let me add) shrewdness of his moral teaching and the rampant megalomania which must lie behind his theological teaching unless he is indeed God has never been satisfactorily got over. Hence the non-Christian hypotheses succeed one another with the restless fertility of bewilderment.' These four elements – his character, teaching, powers and claims – must be kept intact and not be artificially fragmented. If they aren't kept together, we are not giving Jesus due deference for being God or acknowledging him on his own terms. We are not even being honest about the evidence before us.

When we put it all together, the claims of Jesus to be God are seen to be just what we would expect. If Someone from a higher order has broken into our world, then we should expect him to possess a peerless – and often surprising – moral character. We would expect, also, that he would see life with a clarity and a perception that we could never match; we would expect him to be able to communicate such insights to us. It goes almost without saying that he would possess remarkable powers, especially against the ills of this world order.

If he had all that, then we should be very surprised if he did not either directly or indirectly tell us from time to time who he was and where he came from. This is precisely what Jesus did.

2
History in the making

JESUS WAS A REAL MAN. He was no myth or legend, no 'nice little story' invented to illustrate religious ideas or ideals. He was part of the genuine, factual history of the world. The Gospels – the four accounts of Jesus' life that we have in the New Testament – are *history* books.

But they are history of a highly *selective* kind. Not everything that Jesus did is recorded in them – nor everything that was happening in the world of his day. Particular events illustrating his message are set down. Special attention is given to the last week of Jesus' life – to his execution and resurrection. A Gospel is not just history (dates, facts and figures), but 'good news'.

A selective history

The whole of the Bible is concerned with history. In fact, it claims that the almighty, invisible God has revealed himself in and through its history. He is not a God who stays 'up there' in some remote spiritual world. He comes 'down' into this world to judge and to rescue. This process began in ancient times (recorded in the Old Testament) and found its completion in the life of Jesus. With his birth into history 'the Word was made flesh and dwelt among us' (John 1:14).

The four accounts of Jesus' life resemble other histories and yet are unlike them. They describe events that do not normally happen. For example, the Gospels tell of Jesus using God's power to heal needy people. The 'end' of Jesus' life is one of the biggest surprises of all!

The Gospel writers were also aware that they were not writing about an ordinary person. Jesus was 'God invading his own creation' as a human being. And yet the writers don't push their histories into some special 'religious' sphere. They move easily from the natural to the supernatural – just as Jesus did.

Take, for example, one of the Gospel writers, Luke. He wrote just like any other historian:

❑ He collected his data from what was handed on by eyewitnesses of Jesus' life.
❑ He made an independent investigation of all this material, putting it into a connected narrative.
❑ He crafted a cohesive but authentic history, shaping his account to suit his overall themes.

Today with our dependence on large reference libraries with their well-kept material (including even films and tape-recordings), we tend to forget how accurately the ancient world preserved and passed on its own history. Because many people could not read or write, they cultivated their memories, constantly checking each other for accuracy and then eventually having scribes record what was said. It was as reliable a method as any that has appeared since their time.

History with a purpose

The Gospel writers did not write for the curious, nor give information for information's sake. Without tampering with the facts of Jesus' life and teaching, they arranged this information to commend him to others.

All historians write from a particular point of view, whether economic, political, social or from some other slant. Also each has his or her own unique perspective. Each from the sum total of his own experience and preference sees the data through his own eyes. This does not make him or her inaccurate or untrustworthy – unless he distorts or hides the historical material. It simply means that the historian is personally involved. For this reason any modern historian who was not open to the possibility of the supernatural would be unable to write the Gospels because he could not understand Jesus as he actually was.

Is it legitimate to write history from a personal point of view? Yes, because all history writers do it.

Were the Gospel writers 'biased'? Yes, but they claimed their convictions were given to them by God's Spirit, thus giving them the true inside story of Jesus. The Gospel writers would say – and no one has any way of proving them wrong – that the phenomenon called Jesus was so remarkable that no group of people could have clubbed together to invent it.

Compare Jean-Jacques Rousseau: 'It is more inconceivable that several men should have united to forge the gospel than that a single person should have furnished the subject of it. The gospel has marks of truth so great, so striking, so perfectly inimitable, that the inventor of it would be more astonishing than the hero.'

All this has a special application to the contemporary seeker. The Christian claim is that, if our minds are also open to God's Spirit, we too shall see Jesus as he really is and respond to him. This explains how people, when reading the Gospels, suddenly find that the whole story comes alive for them. It is as if God himself removes the veil of scepticism and they find themselves, like Peter, John or Matthew in the Gospel story, rising to follow Jesus no matter where it may lead.

The word 'history' suggests time and space, date and place. Like the cross-hairs in a gunsight, they create a 'fix' for events on history's time-line. The letters BC and AD have become a measuring stick for all times and dates.

'When the time had fully come, God sent his Son, born of a woman,' wrote the apostle Paul (Galatians 4:4). What a time it was – perhaps easier for us to see in hindsight than for many of those who were part of it! In this period various important influences emerged which, without any collusion, combined to prepare the way for Jesus.

Three of these influences were the Jewish, Roman and Greek worlds. We will examine each of them in turn.

At the right time, in the right place
(a) The Jewish world
On the eastern shores of the Mediterranean Sea is

Palestine. It forms a land-bridge between the three continents of Europe, Asia and Africa – a natural starting point for the worldwide spread of Christianity. The people who lived there – the Israelites – had in their religious tradition a natural starting point for it as well. Jesus, born a Jew, inherited the fruits of the years of tuition through which his people had passed. He had no need to waste time correcting polytheism (the worship of many gods) or idolatry (the worship of false gods), nor did he need to teach the importance of high ethical standards. He inherited Temple and synagogue worship. The latter had a profound effect on the new churches that sprang up when the Christian message went international.

Jesus stepped into a scene where the Jewish hope of the coming Messiah or world king was burning brighter than it had done for centuries. Of course, Jesus sought to reform, refine and revolutionise much in Jewish religion. But there was no nation under heaven that could have provided a better base for what he had come to do and say. As Jesus himself was to say to a semi-pagan woman in Samaria, 'Salvation is from the Jews' (John 4:22).

(b) The Roman world

In the Romans, Christianity found a strange ally. Roman help was at first indirect – through the kind of society which it had created. But, three hundred years after Jesus was born, Christianity would enter into formal marriage 'for better or for worse' with the Roman Empire.

The law and order that the Romans imposed on the world proved essential. The Roman legions had subdued an enormous territory and a varied collection of nations. For the Empire to endure, it was imperative that the world be unified. The Caesars and their administrators worked hard to make it so. The *Pax Romana* (Roman peace) made the world a safer place to travel in. It cleared the way for the rapid spread of ideas and religions. With the Roman peace went Roman roads, opening up lines of communication with far-flung places and providing a ready-made path for the gospel.

(c) The Greek world

The Empire also provided a common language. The Roman overlords had been influenced by the culture and literature of the empire they subdued. Everywhere in the civilised world could be found the influence of the Greeks. People were often bilingual, speaking Greek as well as their own tongue. This universal language, so flexible and expressive, was crucial for a message which was soon to see itself in international terms. Indeed the very Gospels which tell the story of Jesus, together with the rest of the New Testament, were originally written in Koine or colloquial Greek.

An uncertain world

There were other influences. For one thing, many people had a sense of insecurity. Many were uprooted from their own culture. Millions were slaves – two out of every three people in the city of Rome, for example. Even those who led a more favoured existence found the Empire big and impersonal. They longed for a faith that would give them self-respect, a purpose in life, and a sense of belonging to a group of like-minded people.

With this came a deep moral and spiritual hunger. The notion that the ancient world was innocent and inwardly secure is untrue. A more accurate picture was given by St Paul when he wrote to Christians living in Rome itself. He set down a catalogue of spiritual darkness, moral corruption and inhumanity (Romans 1:24-32) – the real picture of the times in which they lived. Of course there were some who were revolted by the times and longed for a better way. However, the very gods they were supposed to worship were not as moral as the best mortals of the period. Intelligent people could only hold to their religious faith if they treated it as a myth.

So the old gods had lost their power. A desperate attempt was made to fill the vacuum with new gods imported from the east or with the worship of the Caesar. But if somebody could have offered a faith that dealt with the nagging sense of guilt and offered a high moral standard, the ancient world would have been ready to listen. If that faith also offered hope beyond the grave, it would have been doubly intriguing.

Jesus came to answer all of these longings. He taught a higher standard of ethics than the world had ever seen, but he did so with the guarantee that God's own Spirit would enable us to fulfil it. He dealt with sin and guilt not by sweeping them under the carpet, but by exposing them. Through the cross, he made it possible for us to approach God with a freed conscience. Through his resurrection he overcame humanity's last enemy, death. In calling people into fellowship with himself, he created a loving community, offering acceptance and significance to all. Without doubt Jesus and his message had come when the time was ripe.

Frozen in time?

Perhaps some may be prepared to accept the historicity of Jesus and to recognise the aptness of the *time* of his coming, but in doing so find themselves with another problem: if all this happened so long ago (and far away) what has it got to do with us now? If in Jesus God was invading our world, why can't he do so again? Why did he lock himself into one time and one place: first-century Palestine?

The answer is 'He can and yet he can't!' In order to be truly historical, he had to be limited to one time and place. God is no exception to his own rule. God had revealed himself in nature – and still does. Further, God revealed himself through the teachings of the Old Testament prophets and the New Testament apostles. But it is as the man Jesus that he has revealed himself most definitively.

The process of showing himself to humanity began in the great saving events of the Old Testament, but found its climax in Jesus. In him God made a *personal* appearance.

God cannot leave us to discover what we can

about him from nature alone, as Israel's neighbours did in their cruel and morally corrupt religions. Nor can he leave us to the vagaries of our own thoughts and ideas. He must be more specific because we so easily twist and modify spiritual truth to suit our own ends and make for ourselves gods which are as tame, manageable and self-serving as we are. God had to spell out for us the essential truth about himself and do this *once and for all*. Only then could we be sure that we are in touch with the real God and are not simply projecting our own mental image onto him.

However, Jesus' coming was for all time and for all generations. By becoming representative man, he has caught up into himself all those who lived before he came and all those who have lived since.

This is especially true of that most crucial event: his death and resurrection. In his dying, all died; in his rising, all rose. In representing us and taking our place on the cross, it is *as if* we were there and were executed for our wrongdoing. In rising from the dead, Jesus has lifted us up with him beyond sin and its condemnation to make us part of his magnificent new creation. Here sin, death and sorrow have no part.

The ever-present God

It may be argued that, even if this is true, our participation in Christ's death and resurrection takes place in the unseen spiritual realm. I remain part of this world, still besieged by its ills and evils. This is true. But Jesus promised before he left the world – and many have found his promise true – that he would send his Spirit into the hearts and lives of those who accept him and make him their Lord. His Spirit is the one in whom God's future kingdom becomes a present reality, giving us a sample of what is in store for us.

So, although God could come as he did in Jesus once and for all, it is quite clear that in his Spirit he can come to us *all the time.* The limitations that Jesus put himself under in first-century Palestine no longer apply. He may – and does – enter a relationship with anyone anywhere regardless of time and place, but he brings with him the unique benefits that he won for us on the cross. It is because he was prepared to be limited *then* that his blessings are unlimited *now.*

3

The Jesus story

ONE OF THE MOST REMARKABLE features in the history of literature is the record of Jesus' life. There is nothing like it in all the writings of the past.

No one else from so long ago has been as clearly described. His personal characteristics, his actions, his conversations and his teachings are so plainly recorded that he comes across as a real and vivid personality. As we have seen, the Gospel writers did not need to invent anything: they simply told the amazing story of Jesus as it was.

The amount of space that they gave to various aspects of Jesus' life is a message in itself. There are a few birth stories, one brief account of an event from his childhood and then virtual silence – until we come to the commencement of his ministry.

Then the full details begin: there are three years of intensive activity, of teaching and healing, of controversy and the making of claims. Then a great deal of space – nearly a third of the whole of the Gospels – is given to Jesus' last week on earth and, in particular, to his death and his resurrection.

Early beginnings

There's a lot more that we could put together on the life of Jesus by guesswork and imagination. Jesus' parables give us *some* insight into his everyday life: in the home, the field and the marketplace. His use of nature illustrations take us out onto the hills around Nazareth where perhaps he went for times of quiet and prayer. We go with him to the local synagogue (Luke 4:16-22).

We know that Jesus could read and write (John 8:6). Even from early years he had an amazing grasp of spiritual truth (Luke 2:46-47). But overall the Gospel writers do not give much space to these details. They show us by their selection of material that Jesus' ministry – especially his death and resurrection – is where the focus of our faith should be.

Jesus' entry into the world was almost like a foretaste of what was to come. 'There was no place . . . in the inn' (Luke 2:7) – and there would later be no room for him in many a human heart. And yet some were glad to see him. He received a welcome from the *workers* – the shepherds, true representatives of the ordinary people of the day. He received a welcome from the *wise*, those mysterious magi who came from the East because of their semi-scientific investigations. Jesus was also welcomed in the Jewish Temple by *worshippers* – the devout people who spent their days in earnest prayer for God to break the silence of the centuries and send his Messiah.

It was in that same Temple that Jesus, as a twelve-year-old, would astound the professional theologians and astonish his parents with his remarkable awareness of God as his Father. With these few scant references to his early life, there is a silence of some eighteen years.

Jesus and cousin John

When Jesus came on the scene again, it was in connection with the formidable figure of John the Baptist. They were in fact related to each other. John, too, was an unusual child with an important future. He disappeared into the solitude of the desert, eventually emerging in the fifteenth year of the Roman emperor Tiberius (about AD 28-29). He came as 'the voice of one crying in the wilderness' (Matthew 3:3). He had opted for an alternative to the soft and easy life – he wore a camel's hair cloak and ate rough desert food – but he spoke with the voice of prophetic authority so long silent in Israel.

John's message was simple, but demanding: people must escape God's coming judgment and prepare for his coming kingdom by turning away from their sins and accepting baptism as a sign of cleansing. (His hearers had seen pagans baptised into the Jewish faith. John, by offering them baptism, was virtually saying that their sins and formal religion had put them outside of Israel. Also their baptism in water was a preparation for something greater still: baptism with the Holy Spirit.)

Jewish people felt that the Spirit's presence had been absent for many years, though there were promises in the Old Testament that one day he would come upon them in mighty power.

From river to desert

People responded warmly to John's preaching. The religious officials did not approve, but ordinary people came from all over Palestine to listen and be baptised. Among them, much to John's embarrassment, was Jesus!

John recognised him as the Coming One for whom he was preparing the way. Why did Jesus need to be baptised? Shouldn't Jesus perhaps baptise John himself? But no. Jesus had come into this world to be identified with sinful humanity. He would later be called the 'friend of publicans and sinners', taking their sins upon his own head when he went to the cross. So now he decided to be baptised with the crowds – with the soldiers, the taxgatherers, the prostitutes and all the other riff-raff just as if he were one of them.

A most remarkable thing happened at Jesus' baptism: God's power came upon him visibly and audibly. The Holy Spirit descended on him like a dove and God's voice came to him with words of acceptance and commendation. It was his call to leave the silent obscurity of Nazareth and begin his public ministry. He was now assured of his task. He was now equipped for his task. He was now committed to his task.

The first movement of the Spirit was to drive Jesus out into the Judean desert – to be put to the test at the subtle hands of the Devil! The rest of Jesus' ministry would be a pitched battle with the forces of evil; this engagement was the first part of the campaign. The lines of battle were being drawn before taking the attack into enemy territory.

The point at issue in the Tempter's threefold assault was the appeal to compromise – to gain the right ends by the wrong means. In his ministry, Jesus would be faced with great opportunities but also great opposition. It was vitally important that, before he began, he should clear away all indecision or uncertainty about how he would make his approach to the people.

❑ The first temptation – to turn the stones into bread – was an appeal to the *material* rather than the spiritual, to offer a programme which would fill people's bellies, but leave them inwardly unsatisfied.

❑ The second temptation – to cast himself down from the Temple – was an appeal to the *spectacular*, to win people by cheap tricks and dazzling displays, yet once again leave them unchanged.

❑ The third temptation – to worship the Devil so as to win the world – was an appeal to *compromise*, to drop the high demands of discipleship and adopt surrounding society's easy-going, self-centred ways.

Jesus answered all three temptations with apt quotations from his Bible and by unswerving loyalty to God himself. He refused the subtle insinuation that he might not be God's Son or that he might not have been called by God: '*If* you are God's Son . . .' He refused to take the easy way out and modify his message so as to fit it in with others' expectations.

In this he was refusing the path which would eventually avoid the cross. He knew that the Devil's appealing alternative programmes would leave us as we are: unsatisfied, unchanged and unredeemed. By facing these temptations head-on, Jesus learnt to feel for us in our temptations and to help us through them.

From obscurity to popularity

We know little of Jesus' first year of ministry. It has been called 'the year of obscurity'. It seems at first that he stayed in Judea, his ministry overlapping with John the Baptist's. Jesus' disciples were also baptising, indeed winning more followers than John – a fact the religious authorities found somewhat unnerving, but which John gladly accepted.

When John's outspoken criticism of the morals of Prince Herod resulted in him being arrested, Jesus saw it as a sign that his days of preparation were obviously over. So Jesus made his way back to Galilee to begin his life's work.

In Galilee Jesus had grown to manhood. It was the region he knew best and was heavily populated, filled with towns and villages. The Galileans themselves were less conservative, more open to new ideas with the constant flow of trade and traders through their territory. The Jewish historian, Josephus, described them as a people open to change and ever ready for revolutionary leaders. It is not surprising, then, that Jesus' second year of ministry has been called 'the year of popularity'.

There were three main elements in Jesus' public ministry. First, there was his *teaching and preaching.* He made a broad appeal to the populace, talking in synagogues, in the open air or wherever he could get a hearing, raising and answering questions as he did so. He gave time to his disciples, as well as to the crowds, spelling out the characteristics of God's kingdom.

He did not merely quote others, nor was he satisfied merely to speak in God's name as the prophets had done. He spoke in his own name and in such a way as to convince his hearers that he knew what he was talking about. By his use of parables he put heaven and earth side-by-side, calling ordinary people to decision and commitment in terms that they could understand.

Second, Jesus met *people's needs,* especially in his healing of the mind and body. To Jesus, disease was an unwelcome intruder into God's good creation: it was not part of God's original plan, nor part of his final one.

Jesus was no wonder-worker intent on impressing the crowd with spectacular tricks. However, his healing and his teaching were part-and-parcel of each other. As he announced the coming of God's kingdom, so he illustrated it with 'signs'. The healings were 'audio-visual aids' designed to demonstrate that what Jesus was teaching had actually occurred. They showed God's kingdom of love had invaded enemy territory – that the forces of evil were now in retreat and would one day be banished altogether and that God himself was at work amongst men and women, touching and healing the spiritual and physical evils which prevented them from being whole persons.

The third aspect of Jesus' ministry was forced upon him: *controversy with the religious officials.* Jesus was just as concerned about righteousness as they but, whereas they stressed the meticulous keeping of the letter of the law, he went for its inner meaning. Calling for a childlike sincerity and liberty in obeying the heavenly Father, Jesus warned against the formalism and hypocrisy of legalism. By associating with many whom the officials considered spiritual outcasts, he also attacked their exclusive attitudes. Jesus went so far as to forgive the sins of these outsiders, thus opening himself up to the charge of blasphemy – a charge which would one day be used to condemn him to death.

Magic or madness?

Another point of controversy was Jesus' power to heal. His critics challenged him to produce a sign from heaven to demonstrate that his powers came from God. When he refused, his critics inferred that his power came from elsewhere – that he was a sorcerer. Or else it was suggested, even by his relatives, that he was out of his mind!

So as Jesus' popularity grew the opposition also grew. Many Galileans became his true disciples, giving themselves to following his teachings. The crowds also grew, but Jesus became increasingly dissatisfied with their response. They lacked real repentance and genuine faith. They were glad when he fed them or when he appeared to be the long-awaited leader. But the Galileans resisted any inward change in themselves or any transformation of their values.

From among Jesus' followers, an inner circle was formed. This core-group of disciples was deeply committed to Jesus, accompanying him on his preaching journeys. These twelve apostles became the foundation of the new Israel, just as the twelve patriarchs in the Old Testament had founded the original Israel.

The apostles were a motley crew. They included four fishermen, one tax collector, at least one revolutionary and a person who would prove to be a traitor. But Jesus shared himself with them at a deep and personal level, training them and equipping them for their future unique leadership role in the Christian church.

The Galilean crowds meanwhile grew and grew. The high point of Jesus' popularity – and also a critical point in his ministry – was when, with very few resources, he fed the five thousand. It was his last attempt to get the Galileans to understand his message, but they did not do so. They were impressed all right with his potential as a revolutionary leader, but Jesus would not become their kind of messiah: someone to oust the Romans and make Israel great again. Jesus withdrew into the hills by himself and the crowd dispersed.

The turning point
The third and last year of Jesus' ministry has been called 'the year of adversity'. He appears to have

avoided Galilee, preaching in more distant places. No doubt the opposition had become more intense as professional theologians came to Galilee from Jerusalem. Herod, too, it was said, was out to kill him as he had John the Baptist.

So we find Jesus in his final year spending more time with his disciples. Eventually, he tested them. After discussing various popular views, he asked *them* who they thought he was? Peter answered: 'the Christ'. This concise answer was a critical turning-point in Jesus' career. He began to speak about the need to go to Jerusalem, the centre of Israel's faith, and about the violent death that he would experience there. From this time Jerusalem, imminent death and his inevitable resurrection were his constant themes.

In the next six months Jesus actually made a number of visits to Jerusalem to test the atmosphere of the city. On one occasion, after addressing the crowds in the Temple, he barely escaped with his life! He knew now beyond all shadow of doubt what awaited him – and he made his plans accordingly.

He timed his approach to Jerusalem for the Passover season, March or April. The city would then be crowded with pilgrims, so his challenge to the authorities would be made before the widest possible audience. His death at this time would provide the new sacrifice which would create the new people of God – just as the Passover released God's people from Egypt. Whilst Jesus was eventually to be the victim of a gross miscarriage of justice, the decision to go to Jerusalem was his.

Hour of destiny

Jesus' final approach to the city was made in triumph and tears. At the first sight of the city, he wept over its stony heart – over what might have been if the people had responded to his message. Then, surrounded by shouting pilgrims (perhaps some former Galilean supporters?), he made his triumphal procession into the city. Mounted on a donkey, he fulfilled the ancient prophecy that described the coming of Jerusalem's gentle, peace-bearing king. Yet the city would reject the only one in whom it would have found its peace. Jerusalem opted for armed confrontation and forty years later this decision would surround it with a Roman army which would almost annihilate it.

The next move Jesus made was in the most sensitive area of all. He entered the Temple, expelling the sellers of animal sacrifices and those changing money for foreign pilgrims. This was a direct challenge to the priestly custodians of the Temple who condoned, if not owned, these commercial ventures.

Reletting the family farm

Little wonder that the religious officials demanded to know by what authority Jesus had acted. In giving them an answer, he told them a parable that soon had them plotting his arrest.

It was the story of a landowner (obviously God) who rented his vineyards to tenants (the people of Israel). The landowner sent servants (the prophets) time and again to collect his rightful dues but, when the tenants rejected the servants and ill-treated them, he finally sent his own son. The tenants, sensing that this was their opportunity to take over the property, killed him and threw his body out of the vineyard.

Jesus asked what the owner would do about this and then he answered his own question: he would terminate the first lease and relet the vineyard. There could be no mistaking what Jesus was driving at: he was serving notice on the religious authorities. Because of their high-handed attitudes, God was about to foreclose on his previous agreement with them and enter into a new one with whoever would accept it. The new vineyard, the new Israel, would be under new management.

This was the last straw. The authorities decided they must act quickly. The city was filling fast with pilgrims, some of whom might well be sympathetic to Jesus' cause. If the delicate balance of power by which Judea existed under the Romans was not to be upset, Jesus must be arrested as soon as possible.

But here there was a problem. If Jesus were to be apprehended publicly, there would be a riot. As the hunters anxiously stalked their prey, their problem was solved. One of Jesus' own disciples, Judas, offered to lead them to him by night and they were able to take him with little or no trouble. Jesus was now on his way to execution.

4

The kingdom of God

GREAT MOVEMENTS IN HISTORY are often able to put their message into a catchphrase. For the French revolutionaries it was 'Liberty, equality and fraternity'. For the drafters of the American constitution it was 'government of the people, by the people, for the people'. For twentieth century political leaders it has been 'the New Deal', 'the Great Society', 'the Welfare State' or 'the Just Society'. For Jesus it was 'the kingdom of God'.

Jesus spoke about the kingdom all the time. He began his ministry by saying: 'The time is fulfilled, the kingdom of God is at hand; repent and believe the gospel' (Mark 1:15). Just before he farewelled his disciples he was still speaking about it (Acts 1:3). In fact, he said that to preach the good news of the kingdom was the reason for his coming into the world (Luke 4:43). The kingdom had been John the Baptist's message, too. He had warned the people of his day that, unless they repented, God's kingdom would burst upon them and take them by surprise.

'The kingdom is here'
The phrase 'kingdom of God' (or Matthew's

equivalent phrase 'kingdom of heaven') is used nearly 120 times in the Gospels. Everywhere Jesus went it was his main message. His most characteristic form of teaching, the parable, often has the kingdom of God as its theme.

John the Baptist saw himself as preparing the way for the Lord and his coming kingdom. This was to be a time when God would sift and cleanse his people through judgment and repentance. A central part of his message was to warn people to watch for the Coming One who would personify that kingdom.

When Jesus came on the scene, John was content to see his own disciples abandon him to follow Jesus. Although Jesus took over John's message, he had a broader approach than John. He, too, stressed judgment and the need for repentance, but he had a stronger emphasis on the liberating power of the kingdom. He declared that the kingdom was already present in the world – in his helping, healing and preaching.

'Are you the One?'

Later on, when he was languishing in prison, John the Baptist went through a dark period when he began to doubt that Jesus was indeed the Coming One. Jesus sent him a reassuring message. In his speech and action all the qualities that the prophets had signposted were coming to pass: disabled people were being healed; the poor were hearing the good news; even the dead were being raised to life.

What did Jesus mean by the phrase 'the

kingdom of God'? It was certainly an expression which was well-known to the people of his day. They had a great hope that some day God would break into history and restore their national fortunes. The messiah, the anointed king, would come to re-establish the throne of David and so prepare the way for the coming of God's kingdom.

Sometimes they saw it all in a nationalistic way, sometimes as a great supernatural event which would renew the world. Whichever way, they had distorted the original vision of the prophets – they had politicised the phrase 'kingdom of God', reducing it to a slogan for Jewish nationalism.

'Give us a strong man'

It was nationalistic ideas like these that drove the crowds, during the popular phase of Jesus' ministry, to try to make him king by force. Their hopes had no doubt been raised by Jesus continually stressing the coming of God's kingdom. But he had rejected such political offers when he had been tempted in the wilderness and he was not about to change his mind. Instead, he stepped up the challenging aspects of his teaching until the ranks of his shallower followers began to thin out.

Even his inner circle (the disciples) were shaken. They, too, found it hard to get worldly ideas of the kingdom out of their heads. On one occasion a couple of them tried to wangle themselves the top places in the kingdom. Jesus explained by washing their feet what true leadership was all about – it meant being a servant to all. Even after Jesus' resurrection, they still expected to see him set up some kind of political regime (Acts 1:6).

The coming age
With such ideas floating around, it must have been a temptation for Jesus to drop the idea of the kingdom altogether! But he was too familiar with the Bible (the Old Testament) to do that. Israel's prophets had painted such an inviting picture of the new age to come, bracing in its stark simplicity, that it would have been impossible for Jesus to avoid making this his main message. There would be, said the prophets, a time of peace, prosperity and justice. Sickness would be eradicated. Nature would be so transformed that even lions and lambs would lie down together. People would be given a new heart under the influence of God's own Spirit and the true knowledge of the true God would spread everywhere. It was a hope that could never be abandoned by anyone who loved the Old Testament and took it seriously.

But humanity has the fatal ability to take hold of beautiful things and twist and distort them out of all recognition. Despite his contemporaries' politicising of the prophetic vision, Jesus made the kingdom of God his central theme, rejecting or correcting most of what the people of his day said about it. His was an uncompromising message based on a clear perception of God's plan for a creative, purposeful, richly textured society.

God's rule begins
How, then, did Jesus bring in the kingdom of God?

There were three distinct stages:

1. The kingdom had come with Jesus. When some Pharisees demanded to know *when* the kingdom would arrive, he said it was 'in the midst' of them already. Jesus' ability to heal, cast out demons and control a storm – even to bring the dead back to life – were clear evidence that God's kingdom had arrived in visible form.

2. Jesus had broken the self-perpetuating cycle of evil. When Jesus cast out demons, he was breaking into the Devil's domain, rescuing those who had been spiritually imprisoned. The focus of his attack was the Devil's ultimate power and authority. Jesus could only release people from demonic influence because he had overthrown the enemy's supreme command.

3. Jesus proclaimed the good news to 'the poor'. Jesus' message, the gospel, was for all who were desperately conscious of their need of God's grace and forgiveness. His preaching was a living demonstration that no one need wait any longer for the kingdom. Jesus was here. The kingdom was also here.

A riddle . . . and its answer

There are two puzzling aspects to Jesus' teaching about the kingdom:

(a) Why, if the kingdom came, was it not more obvious? True, Jesus helped, healed, fed and forgave people. But he did not do this for everyone. Even when he had risen from the dead, life went on as usual: people hurt each other, they got sick and died, they ignored God, great human problems like poverty and injustice continued. *Where* was the kingdom? Where is it now?

(b) Why did Jesus, after stressing so strongly that the kingdom had come, still speak about it as if it was in the *future*? Indeed, in the Lord's Prayer, he taught his disciples to pray this way ('Your kingdom *come*').

The answer to each of these two questions is basically the same. Although the kingdom had come, it had come only provisionally. It was here, but not *fully* here. Jesus' own coming into the world was a two-stage affair:

❑ His first coming was in great humility. Born into a peasant family in the backblocks of the Roman Empire, he lived as a village carpenter, then as an itinerant preacher. Finally he allowed himself to be executed as a common criminal amid human contempt.

❑ His second coming will be when he returns again in majesty and triumph. Then he will judge humanity, transforming the universe.

At Jesus' first coming, the kingdom was established in a mysterious and hidden form. The King himself consented to become the servant of humanity – to live without property or even a resting place. There was a hiddenness about him just as there is about his kingdom. This actually fits in very well with the nature of God's kingdom. It is not 'obvious': it is without the pomp or trappings of earthly government. Instead it is a kingdom based on love, sacrifice and humility.

When John the Baptist could not quite see this, Jesus told him not to be 'offended' at the way the kingdom had come. The kingdom was there for those who had eyes to see it.

Mysterious growth
Jesus' parables of growth help explain the mysterious nature of the kingdom.

❑ It is like *seed* sown in various soils. People have a mixed reaction to the King. They still have the freedom to oppose him.

❑ The kingdom is like a *field* in which God and his Enemy have both sown seed. Good and bad grow side-by-side, only to be sorted out at the end of time.

❑ It is like a pinch of *yeast* mixed into a loaf. It begins small – in the response of individual human hearts – but its eventual form will be immense and pervasive.

Perhaps because the kingdom has this element of mystery about it, Jesus did not define it. He preferred analogies to definitions, describing what the kingdom of God was 'like' (a word often used to introduce the parables of the kingdom). How could an all-wise, all-loving, all-powerful God direct and control a world in which so many evil things continue to exist? How can God's kingdom have come if people still oppose God the King? Jesus' parables give us the clues.

'Your kingdom come'
The very phrase 'kingdom of God' suggests two things: that God is a King; that we are his subjects. His kingdom is not political, so it cannot be found on a map. It is rather his rule, his dominion or

sovereignty. In fact, the parallel phrase to 'Your kingdom come' in the Lord's Prayer is 'Your will be done on earth as it is in heaven'. So God's kingdom is revealed wherever and whenever his will is done among us – as it is amongst angels and the redeemed in heaven.

Because of our many imperfections we will never, of course, see God's will done perfectly in this world – until the end comes and the universe is transformed. When Jesus was here physically, God's kingdom was 'earthed' amongst us. In him we see what the kingdom will be like in all its fullness: a world without sickness, sadness or death; a world without guilt, hunger or any sense of estrangement from God and others; a world where love, peace and justice are the ruling principles.

When Jesus came, the kingdom came to *stay*. God's rule or Lordship over us has become a reality. It is established in our lives when our hearts and minds are brought into submission to Jesus. The very fact that our unruly wills and desires can be brought under his gracious control is a sure sign that the whole world will eventually do his will. What a hope for the future! What an encouragement in the present!

A warm welcome

Entry into God's kingdom is a *gift*. We cannot force our way in or earn ourselves a visa by good behaviour. God generously invites us to enter. His invitation is as wide as the world itself. There are those whose pride and stubbornness prevent them from accepting his call. Then the invitation goes to others – to some of the most unlikely people one can imagine.

Jesus, in teaching this and living it out, scandalised many of his critics. He warned the religious people of his day that their smug self-sufficiency was keeping them out of God's kingdom. He further offended them by welcoming the riffraff of society: shifty tax-gatherers, brazen prostitutes and other 'disreputable' people. Realising their need, they readily received the kingdom as a gift, whilst their 'betters' stood outside it and tut-tutted at the company that Jesus kept.

Because Jesus welcomed outcasts, it would be easy to think that life in the kingdom is lax and easygoing. This is not so. In fact, the kingdom makes very strong demands upon us.

The lifestyle of the kingdom, therefore, is different to ordinary human standards. A brief look at the Sermon on the Mount reveals such astonishing values as: forgiving one's enemies, showing active goodwill to all kinds of people regardless of personal preference, having an inner purity of motive, displaying no ostentation in our works or worship, rejecting materialism and refusing to be anxious about making ends meet.

Such attitudes turn ordinary human values upside down (or perhaps 'right side up'!). These standards appear daunting – until we remember that not only our entry into God's kingdom, but also our on-going life in it is by his grace and forgiveness. We can never perfectly fulfil these high aims and will always be in need of forgiveness, but they remain the principles on which the kingdom is based, the compass-point by which we steer our lives.

A hard slog

Because the standards of God's kingdom run contrary to society's, we can expect conflict and suffering. When Jesus raided the Devil's realm, he set in motion a supernatural battle. But, although surrounded by fierce opponents to God's control, his kingdom is here to stay and will win in the end.

There are many obstacles in the path of those who would enter the kingdom. For example, money and possessions can be a great hindrance. These baubles often encourage a quite false spirit of independence that imagines that it can manage quite well without God. Material possessions give people a short-sighted view of life that fixes their attention on the tangible but temporary, rather than on eternal realities.

A word to waverers

Indecisiveness is also a great obstacle to entry into the kingdom. There were many in Jesus' day – and many since – who have been unable to commit themselves wholeheartedly to him. Some refuse his invitation point-blank. More neglect it or try to postpone it. Some try to have one foot in the kingdom and one in the world.

To all such waverers Jesus said entry into the kingdom is a matter of extreme urgency. It is not something people can drift into or take up as a part-time hobby. It is something that must be *sought* – made the supreme object of life. We must be prepared to make any sacrifice necessary to become citizens of God's kingdom (Mark 9:43-48)!

As one of Jesus' parables says, the kingdom is like the most perfect pearl in the world – but with an enormous price tag. For the merchant who sought it, the treasure cost all that he had, but for him its purchase meant the end of a lifetime of searching. For those who would enter the kingdom today the cost – and the rewards – are exactly the same.

5

Life in the kingdom

WHEN PEOPLE TODAY use the word 'Christian', they often have a vague if approving picture in mind. They see a kind, gentle and loving person, despite what that person's religious convictions (or lack of them) happen to be.

'Oh, she's a real Christian,' they say. 'She'd do anything for you.'

Yet, is this what Jesus taught? Is that all a Christian is supposed to be – kind and thoughtful? Did Jesus give us a clear picture of how a citizen should live in God's kingdom?

Jesus certainly taught people. Forty-one out of the fifty-nine times that the word 'teacher' is used in the New Testament, it refers to him. He had disciples – the technical term for a 'school' of people who attached themselves to a rabbi. Jesus taught others as well – from a congregation in a synagogue to crowds gathered in the open air. What, then, did Jesus teach us about how we should live?

Jesus' ministry began with the declaration that with him the kingdom of God had arrived. The only response to this was to enter into an entirely new relationship with God: to 'repent and believe the gospel'. This gospel was the good news that God was here, now.

God had not, of course, ever been 'away' from the world he had made; he had never ceased to rule it or enter into people's lives. But there had been times in history when he had made his presence felt with great power and effect. The most crucial of all such times was when Jesus himself was born into the world. Then God paid us a personal visit in human form.

When changing your mind is OK

Often in his parables Jesus suggested that, with his coming, 'zero hour' had arrived and that his hearers must now take decisive action. God was confronting them, demanding to know what they were going to do about it. The response expected of them is plain: they must *repent* and accept the good news that had been announced to them.

To 'repent' means to have a complete change of mind. It means to alter the whole direction of our life: to make radical adjustments in our purposes and plans – our hopes, dreams and habits. Repentance, in fact, commits us to a completely new pattern of life and behaviour. With it goes *belief*: personal trust in all that Jesus is, and has done, for us. The life that we then live simply flows out of this new relationship with him.

This new lifestyle is not always spelt out in detail by Jesus. Unlike the Greek or Jewish moralists of his day, he did not provide an elaborate set of rules for all occasions. He left a lot to the awakened consciences of those who committed themselves to him. But he does give us some *guidelines* – often in an imaginative, almost poetic way. These help us to apply what Jesus says to all times and all situations without becoming legalistic about it.

Jesus did not, of course, teach in a historical vacuum. He lived in a world where many people had sought long and hard for an ethical way of life. He agreed, and disagreed, with many of the Jewish teachers of his day. In particular, he welcomed their quest for the one great commandment which would simplify the tangled mass of rules and regulations with which they had surrounded themselves. Jesus agreed that by combining two verses from the Old Testament (Deuteronomy 6:5 and Leviticus 19:18) we go right to the heart of what is required of us: to love God with all one's heart and to love one's neighbour as oneself.

These two commandments sum up the essence of Jesus' teaching. But, if we are honest with ourselves, we will immediately recognise that this is much easier said than done. What do these love commandments involve?

The love of God

The world of Jesus' day was filled with gods and other spiritual powers. Some of them, like the gods of the Greeks, were so detached from the world that they would have nothing to do with humanity. They did not get involved with our agonies and struggles. They were 'above' such things in a realm of peace and tranquility. Worse than this, the gods sometimes showed a grudging spirit. They did not wish humanity well and it was rather dangerous for human beings to enjoy too much success or prosperity.

The Jewish idea of God, on the other hand, was of a Being so high and holy that no one, especially those conscious of their sins, would dare approach him. His name was too sacred even to mention.

(a) A God who is near

No one had a higher view of God than Jesus. He knew, as no other person, how pure and morally perfect God is. But the good news, said Jesus, is that this same God is full of kindness and compassion. He is an *inviting* God who calls us to come to him, a *forgiving* God who offers us cleansing from all our sins, and a *seeking* God who goes out after the lost.

Jesus revealed this sort of God. As he said, 'He who has seen me has seen the Father.' Jesus personally welcomed the despised and outcast members of society. He forgave those who were burdened by guilt. He was himself the Good Shepherd who not only sought his lost sheep in the world's wildernesses, but gave his life for them. Every time Jesus showed such kindness and mercy to needy humanity, he laid bare the heart of God.

(b) A God who is dear

Jesus' special word for God was 'Father'. This word had occasionally been used of God in the Old Testament. But Jesus made the term 'Father'

Life in the kingdom

his central title, opening up great new possibilities. From now on it would be possible to have a warm and loving 'family' relationship with God and to know his constant parental care.

Once again, it was Jesus' own example that put content into the word 'Father'. He had a divine sonship, obviously unique. However, expressed in the context of a human life, he left us a workable model to follow. Jesus always spoke to God intimately, addressing him sometimes with the everyday Aramaic word, 'Abba' (Father), used by little children in the home. Following his example, his disciples also used this word, approaching God in the same simple, direct and confident way.

(c) *A God who is there*

Having God as a Father means that he is vitally interested in all our affairs. He is interested in our finances, our health and our emotional well-being, providing all our needs if not always our 'wants'. He loves each of us individually as though there was but one of us to love. Having God as a Father means that we can go to him and talk to him about anything, doing it in a thoroughly natural way. There is no call for formality or elaborate ceremonial. We are coming to a Father.

Love of others

(a) *Like father, like son*

If God is our Father, then other human beings are our brothers and sisters. Differences of race, age or gender are dissolved by the fact that, as Jesus teaches us in the Lord's Prayer, we come to *'our*

Father', not just to my Father.

It is our special relationship with God that helps to explain our responsibility to others. In the Sermon on the Mount, Jesus taught us that Christian behaviour is a case of 'like father, like son'. We must learn to love people the way God does – without bias or prejudice, regardless of what they are like and what their attitude to us is. God sends the benefits of creation (rain and sunshine) on all kinds of people without any distinction.

We, too, must love that way: not simply showing goodwill to relatives and friends – even the worst of people can do that – but showing love to strangers and even enemies. In this way the two great commandments – love for God and love for one's neighbour – meet and match each other. When we love like this we are true children of 'the Most High, for he is kind to the ungrateful and the selfish' (Luke 6:35).

(b) To all and sundry

The law of love is simple, but also very demanding. Loving God involves our whole being: it must be done 'with all your heart, with all your soul and with all your mind'. We must also love our neighbour with the same intensity with which we love ourselves.

Jesus widened the concept of 'neighbour' to include our enemies. In our relationships with each other, we are not to retaliate even when we have a legitimate grievance. We are to be generous to those who defraud us; our forgiveness must be unlimited. Our heavenly Father exhibits these same qualities in his dealings with us. So does Jesus. So, too, must we if we are to follow him.

Paved with good intentions

With teaching so simple yet demanding, Jesus soon found himself in conflict with the moral teachers of his day. He, like them, accepted the law of Moses as authoritative, but his interpretation was quite different. Jesus had no time for their fussy rules and regulations. These not only complicated the law; they often obscured its real meaning.

Jesus' contemporaries, in their attempt at defining the smallest details of the law, often overlooked 'weightier' matters such as justice, mercy and faithfulness. By trying so hard not to infringe the technical restrictions of the law (e.g. healing on the sabbath), they actually found themselves unable to help people in need.

Jesus knew how dangerous such legalism was. By stressing the outward act, one could easily forget the inward attitude. Jesus taught that both good and bad actions originated in the heart. One could commit murder or adultery there. Or one could produce good things like fruit on a good tree. Therefore, we must be people of integrity, whose motives and actions agree with each other and whose goodness comes from the inside out.

Because of his strong emphasis on the heart, Jesus also warned against displaying religion and righteousness. He saw people cleaning up the outsides of their lives while neglecting the corruption within. He saw self-righteous people who had contempt for others. And he saw much hypocrisy: people whose fine words and formal actions were nothing more than an 'act'. (Hypocrisy literally means 'playacting'.)

With his profound insight, Jesus saw deep into the hearts of people and how easily an outer show could cloak a heart unwilling to love God or others. He saw, too, a similar unwillingness to submit to his own claims. He warned people – and conflict erupted.

Despite his deep love and compassion for struggling humanity, Jesus had no soft and idealistic thoughts about humanity. He saw people as 'lost', 'perishing' and in need of God's rescue. He was no sentimentalist, but knew only too well the darker side of human nature. Jesus was well aware of the obstacles that would stand in the path of those who sought to fulfil these two great commandments.

The slaying of love

Since the moral teachers of the day saw righteousness in such a legalistic way, they tended to see sin in terms of broken laws. Whilst Jesus agreed with that in part, he went much deeper. He saw sin in terms of motives and hidden intentions and thus was more rigorous in making people face it.

The 'friend of sinners', as Jesus was so contemptuously called by his critics, did not condone or lightly excuse people's wrong attitudes and actions. Indeed, he exposed sin as an offence against love, rather than the mere breaking of a law. Our rebelliousness drives its lance at the heart of God. It is another nail hammered into Jesus' own hand on the cross.

Jesus saw all too starkly sin's malevolent power to blind and deceive. He also saw the consequences of rejection of God and his way: a bad conscience, evil habits, a hardened heart, withered spiritual faculties, ruined relationships and the dreadful finale of God's judgment.

We have here something of a paradox. Jesus taught that our major responsibility was to love God and to love each other. But he also taught that we *cannot* do that because of a fatal flaw in human nature. If we are to know God at all, we must turn to him and beg forgiveness.

While this in part makes it possible for us to obey him, we still fall far short of his high standards. Jesus *could* reduce his standards – but that would make a mockery of all his teaching. How does God solve this riddle?

The triumph of love

The answer lies in God's own love. His forgiveness and his provision of Jesus as our sin-bearer laid the foundation for a completely new kind of relationship with him. God's forgiveness opens up new dimensions of love – as the woman with a somewhat shady past discovered when Jesus accepted and forgave her. She washed his feet with tears of gratitude and then dried them with her hair. She gave to Jesus the only thing of value that she possessed – a priceless box of ointment.

'She loves much,' said Jesus, 'because she has been forgiven much' (Luke 7:47).

The cleansed conscience has a new ability to see God as Father and thus to respond to him with the happy obedience of a well-loved child. As God's Spirit takes up residence in our hearts, the same kind of love that he shows for us is also shared with our neighbours – even with our enemies. Forgiveness is the golden key that releases love and makes all the difference.

Jesus stressed that God's forgiveness was connected with his own death. When he resolutely set his face towards the cross, Jesus knew that there God's love would more than match the hostility of the Devil and the combined forces of evil. Love would expose sin for what it really is, but love would also win the pitched battle against sin.

Love is our law. Love is the standard by which we are shown to fall short of that law. Love at the cross neutralised the power of evil and provided the remedy for our failure. Love gives us the creative ability to steer a truly Christian course.

One of Jesus' closest friends eventually put it all together in a memorable phrase: 'God *is* love.' John understood Jesus and his teaching very well. We show that we too understand it when our lives are controlled by the law of love.

6

Claims and miracles

MOST PEOPLE HAVE A VERY high regard for Jesus. Even when they do not care much for the church or for Christians, they think well of him. Philosophers, moralists, historians – even some who follow other faiths, like Mohammed or Gandhi – have admired him greatly.

But their 'admiration' has often been conditional – made possible only by drastic editing of what the Gospels actually say about him. Jesus was a great and good man, it is said, but his followers – superstitious and well-meaning men – tried to improve on the story by making him into a god with godlike powers.

Well-meaning sceptics

Yet it is not so easy to isolate, then amputate, Jesus' claims and miracles from the rest of the story. They blend in with other remarkable features of his life, often actually illustrating them.

For example, Jesus' compassionate nature and much of his teaching was closely linked with his healing actions. His central message, the kingdom of God, was often demonstrated by the setting right of some physical disorder. It was as if Jesus was saying: 'In God's kingdom there will be no bent and twisted limbs, no bedridden people – and here is the evidence to prove it!'

Sometimes Jesus' *implicit* claims (e.g. that he was God's Son) were made *explicit*, open, by a demonstration of his powers: he 'speeded up' the natural processes of creation by turning a handful of food into a meal for thousands. This meant that he did quickly what God does constantly in a more leisurely way. By such wonders, Jesus was posing an unavoidable question: 'Who *is* this man who does what God alone can do?'

A life without precedent

We cannot brush the miraculous aside as if it were unimportant. Removing it actually robs the Jesus story of most of its meaning, making it inexplicable. For example, why would Jesus' enemies have tried to kill him *unless* he had embarrassed them by his claims, backing these up with his miracles? Without such tangible proof he would have been too innocuous to bother about.

To patronise Jesus by saying that he is merely a good man and a great teacher does not come to terms with the main thrust of the Gospels, either. Indeed, with this approach we are actually left with as many dilemmas as apparent solutions. As hard as it may be for our age to accept, the Gospels must be allowed to speak for themselves, unmuzzled by our sceptical prejudices. The Gospels are asserting that in Jesus something unprecedented occurred – as unique as the very creation of the universe itself!

The Gospels are warning us not to prejudge the issue, dismissing certain events just because we have never seen them happen. To tamper with the message is to destroy the primary evidence for Jesus.

The Gospels are full of the claims that Jesus made for himself. If you add them all up, they come to the one staggering conclusion: that in Jesus the mighty God, the maker and ruler of the universe, was paying our small planet a personal visit – in a form which we could easily comprehend. When Jesus made his stupendous claims, he often did so in a very subtle, almost oblique way. Though he sometimes made direct claims to be God, he usually left it to those looking on to come to their own conclusions.

Jesus may have done this because what he was claiming was too staggering – not to say shocking – for his original hearers. On more than one occasion they took up stones to kill him, the accepted Jewish way of dealing with blasphemers. Jesus' indirect approach may also have been in line with his usual method of teaching: he liked to give his hearers the opportunity to make their own response to what he said about himself. Blatant claims would have mobilised his enemies into violent action before he was ready, robbing well-disposed people of the chance to accept him for who he really was.

A humble egocentric?

One intriguing aspect of these claims is that Jesus prized humility! He was obviously a humble person, demanding meekness and lowliness from those who became his followers. Yet here we find him placing himself right in the *centre* of what he taught.

He claimed he could satisfy the deepest hunger of the human heart ('I am the bread of life'). He said he came to bring illumination into the dark riddle of human existence ('I am the light of the world'). He claimed that he was the only access to God and the giver of eternal life ('I am the way, the truth and the life'). The Gospels are riddled with similar claims. Indeed, on one occasion Jesus actually referred to himself as *I am*, the divine name by which God had revealed himself to Moses at the burning bush.

To return to our riddle: how could such a humble person make such egocentric claims? C.S. Lewis once said that if you had asked Buddha whether he was the son of Brahma he would have replied: 'My son, you are still in the vale of illusion'. If you had asked Mohammed whether he was Allah, he would first have rent his clothes – then cut off your head! But Jesus consistently claimed that to know, see, believe in, receive, hate or honour him was to do the same to God.

Surely the answer to our riddle is that, when Jesus made his high claims, he believed that he was stating the truth. He was not guilty of arrogance or overstatement. Likewise, when the sceptical Thomas fell at his feet after the resurrection, Jesus showed no embarrassment whatsoever. He accepted Thomas' declaration 'My Lord and my God' as a natural and proper response.

Dangerous claims

When Jesus made such sweeping statements as 'I and my Father are one' and 'he who has seen me has seen the Father', he was obviously claiming a unique relationship with God. He was God's *Son*, having the same nature and being as his Father. Although Jesus taught his disciples to address God as their Father, he never suggested that they were 'sons' in the same sense that he was.

Once again, it was his critics who recognised the unique intimacy that he was claiming for himself when he spoke about his heavenly Father. They tried to kill him because 'he called God his Father, making himself equal with God' (John 5:18). The fact that he 'claimed to be the Son of God' (John 19:7) was part of the accusation that they brought before Pontius Pilate. Indeed, when Pilate heard it, he was terrified. After demanding of Jesus 'Where are you from?', Pilate tried desperately to have him released. He obviously believed that there was substance in Jesus' claims.

Jesus also believed that he was the Son of Man, the Messiah and the mysterious, suffering servant of Isaiah's prophecies. As a matter of fact, he believed himself to be the fulfilment of much of the Old Testament. On one occasion after his resurrection, he took two grief-stricken disciples on a panoramic survey of what was written about him and his crucifixion (Luke 24:26-27).

Special claims

There are two claims which are of special importance:

1. Jesus claimed to *forgive sins*. On each occasion that he did so, the bystanders reached the only conclusion they could have reached: 'Who can forgive sins but God alone?'

2. Jesus claimed that he would *judge the world*. The criterion of judgment would be humanity's attitude to him. Both he and his hearers knew that the Old Testament gave such a prerogative to God alone.

Having placed himself at the centre of his teaching, Jesus naturally expected people to come to him: 'come to me'; 'follow me'; 'come after me'. Jesus called people to sacrifice all – not for some great cause, but for himself. He demanded that they make him the supreme object of their faith and devotion. Just as there were no half-measures to the claims which he made for himself, so there were no half-measures to the demands that he made upon his would-be followers.

Who was Jesus?

The honest reader of the Gospels, faced with Jesus' claims, has some hard questions to answer. For example, what right had Jesus to make such claims? If they had been made by an ordinary mortal, we would assume that he is deceived or a deceiver. Either he would be a megalomaniac, totally absorbed with his own importance and thus totally out of touch with reality. Or else he would be a charlatan, playing a devious game of his own to gain some material advantage, or to boost a sick and dangerous ego.

Jesus does not fit either of these two categories.

He is obviously a sane and balanced personality who has deep insights into the minds and motives of others and thus obviously into his own. In the Gospels he is often the one sane man in a crazy world. The other suggestion that he is a deceiver is preposterous. His ethical standards have never been surpassed. His radical insistence on honesty and integrity and his concerted attack on hypocrisy of all kinds rules out the possibility that he was out to lead people astray.

We have seen that it is not possible to isolate and remove his claims from the Gospels. They – along with the miracles – blend perfectly with the rest of the Jesus story. His claims are the story as much as any other part of it and their removal simply confuses the issue.

Of course, for the reader these questions are not merely academic. If Jesus is who he says he is, then he has the right to make absolute claims on us as well. We cannot dismiss him as a distant figure of history who made claims only on those who lived in his own day. The claims he made were for all time. Because of his resurrection, he is alive today, still pressing his claims upon us. As in the Gospels, the question of his identity is still the major issue.

The miracles of Jesus

Today miracles are as 'out' as, in Jesus' day, they were 'in'. Many would say that this only goes to show how superstitious the ancients were – that if such miracles happened today, we would investigate them and probably disprove them!

However, this argument works both ways. It could also be said that where people sometimes arrogantly feel that all is explained, there is no longer any openness to the unusual or the unexpected. To quote William Barclay: 'There is a kind of rationalism that kills wonder. When wonder is dead, wonderful things cease to happen.'

Although in the Gospels faith was not always the prerequisite for a miracle, there was at least one occasion when Jesus could not do any mighty works 'because of their unbelief' (Matthew 13:58). When people assume they know everything, they are really closing their minds to anything beyond their own experience. The scepticism of the age prevents God from working and therefore people conclude (wrongly) that he cannot work.

There is another common argument against the supernatural. Some say miracles are impossible because they interfere with the laws of nature. But 'impossible' is a dangerous word. In a rapidly changing world, what was once thought impossible is now part of everyday life. The 'laws of nature' simply refer to a sequence of events or reactions that always – as far as we know – happen in a certain way. But, if something contrary to this turns up and is well attested, science simply widens its so-called 'law' to include the exception along with the rule.

If, as the Gospels claim, we are in the presence of the greatest 'exception' of all time, we should expect a few surprises. And if he is indeed Lord of nature, we could expect him to widen the range of nature's laws if he wanted to.

Not easily dismissed

Unless we write the Gospels off as being totally unreliable, we are faced with the fact that the miraculous played a large part in the ministry of Jesus.

As William Neil once wrote: 'One of the basic facts of the historical ministry of Jesus, as recorded on page after page of the Gospel record and one which is given pride of place in the earliest preaching, is that by his power countless pain-ridden, deaf, paralysed, deranged mortals were healed of their diseases, restored to sanity and, in a few cases, brought back to life. At a word, or with a touch, without preliminary diagnosis, medical treatment or convalescence, the sick and maimed and the mentally deranged were made whole.

'No amount of rationalisation can dispose of this. If the Gospel records are not to be dismissed as wholly fraudulent, we have to reckon with someone who had this unique power. The Gospels merely give a handful of detailed cases out of what must have been thousands of cures.'

Although Jesus' miracles are so frequent, he never appears as a mere wonder-worker. He refused to perform 'tricks' for the crowds when they demanded them – nor for King Herod when he also demanded a performance just before Jesus' crucifixion. Jesus had, in fact, decided against this misuse of his powers when, in the wilderness, the Devil tempted him to engage in a spectacular, crowd-pleasing stunt. He later refused to win converts by miraculously feeding them. His messiahship was to be established by other means.

Jesus does not seemed to have ever used his power to convince sceptics. Sometimes he used miracles to confirm the precarious faith of new believers or awaken the latent faith of those who were well-disposed towards him. Miracles were part of the way in which Jesus revealed God to the world. They were 'acted parables' in which the Father's love, compassion, mercy and grace were shown to sick and needy people. When they were performed, people felt that they were in God's presence and were so overcome with astonishment and awe that they were compelled to glorify him.

Jesus' miracles also dramatised his own claims. They showed him to be the One about whom the Old Testament prophets spoke. They showed his great spiritual authority, especially over the evil that hurts and destroys humanity. They revealed that he was able to do what only God could do and that he could meet and satisfy the most pressing human need. Miracles were certainly an integral part of Jesus' message.

Two powerful words

There are two words for miracle in the New Testament. The first, *dunamis*, means 'power'. It indicates that God has made a special entry into the world – into the life of someone others were powerless to help. The other word, *semeion*, means 'sign'. This word gives us a very clear picture of what Jesus' miracles were all about.

When Jesus healed or helped someone, he was doing something of great spiritual significance.

John's Gospel is built around various signs, each showing Jesus fulfilling some particular human need:

❏ Jesus turns water into wine. But he can do more than that: he can replace the old religion of law with the new liberty of the gospel.
❏ Jesus takes a drink of water from a social reject. But he can do more than that: he can provide us with a drink that will quench the raging thirst of the human spirit.
❏ Jesus multiplies a boy's lunch till it feeds a vast crowd. But he can do more than that: he can satisfy the gnawing hunger of the human heart.
❏ Jesus opens the eyes of a man who was blind from birth. But he can do more than that: he can bring illumination to those blinded by pride and prejudice.
❏ Jesus raises his friend Lazarus from the tomb. But he can do more than that: he can bring new life to those who are spiritually and morally dead.

All these miracles are signs of what he did and can still do. They are the acted parables of his life and ministry then and now.

The miraculous is possible

Many people today cannot cope with the idea of the miraculous. They have closed their minds against it because so much has either been 'explained' or 'explained away'. Yesterday's superstitions have either been solved or shelved. Unlike the critics of Jesus' day who had no difficulty in believing in his miracles – they accused him of sorcery, not false pretences – today's critics consider the miracles are a later superstitious addition. They would like to retain Jesus, but with his claims and supernatural wonders stripped away.

However this is not an option. The teaching of Jesus, his character, his claims and his remarkable powers are all of a piece. They are interwoven and interconnected like an intricate tapestry. Remove one thread and the picture becomes distorted. Remove more than one thread and the whole fabric begins to collapse.

A tribesman living in a secluded jungle outpost may well believe that people cannot fly, that all skin is dark, that weapons are only effective when in close range, and that voices only carry as far as earshot. But the day a helicopter lands near him and a white man with a gun and radio steps out, the tribesman has to come to terms with a new and astonishing reality.

Likewise, in Jesus Christ we have a person of a different order who has dramatically entered our world. He has transcended the ordinary laws of human experience and exploded our closed and secure system of thought.

For frightened tribesmen and modern sceptic alike, reality can only break through when there is a thorough change of mind and a new openness to truth. Jesus was God's living truth. His claims declared it; his miracles demonstrated it.

7

The titles of Jesus

AS WE HAVE SEEN, people have often tried to make Jesus in their own image. They have projected onto him their hopes and ideals, sometimes because of something he said or because of something they wished he had said. No doubt this is a roundabout tribute to Jesus, a recognition of the immensity of his person and his mind. People are fascinated by him and what he stands for. They are moved by what they see in him, expressing their admiration for him in terms of their own experience.

Unfortunately, we can't adopt this approach to Jesus. It reverses the whole process of God's revealing of himself to us, ignoring what God is really saying and, instead, tries to use Jesus to tell God what he *ought* to have said! Jesus must be allowed to 'be himself'. We must let the New Testament speak to us about him without any alterations or amendments.

One Lord – many titles

Having said this, the New Testament itself offers a number of interpretations of Jesus which, in a sense, go beyond the outward details of his earthly life. There is more to Jesus than meets the eye. His significance is so immense and multi-faceted that it needs further explanation. These interpretations are *not* ideas projected onto Jesus, but ideas derived from his own teaching, especially as it relates to the Old Testament. These interpretations 'unpack' what was already in Jesus.

The many-sided nature of Jesus' life and teaching can be seen by various descriptive titles in the New Testament (Lord, Son of Man, Saviour, etc.). William Barclay, in his book *Jesus As They Saw Him*, lists forty-two of these. Vincent Taylor, another New Testament scholar, claimed that there were more than fifty.

We have decided to examine just five of the titles chosen by Oscar Cullmann in his book, *The Christology of the New Testament*. He has classified them in the following helpful way:

(a) Titles which refer to the earthly work of Jesus:
The Prophet
The Suffering Servant of God
The High Priest

(b) Titles which refer to the future work of Jesus:
The Messiah
The Son of Man

(c) Titles which refer to the present work of Jesus:
The Lord
The Saviour

(d) Titles which refer to the pre-existence of Jesus:
The Word
The Son of God

1. God's spokesman: Jesus the prophet

Those who were close to Jesus could see that he was in God's confidence. He had remarkable insights into human nature and into the hearts and minds of individuals. He spoke out about what God had told him without regard to his own personal safety and could not be intimidated by anyone – even kings, governors or high ecclesiastical authorities. In other words, Jesus was God's spokesman, his prophet.

The nation into which Jesus was born certainly knew about prophets. Moses, the original architect of Israel's national life, had promised that God would raise up a spokesman like himself who would have God's words 'in his mouth'. As the years passed, this is exactly what happened.

From time to time remarkable men, conscious that God had called and sent them, spoke to their people in his name. Their characteristic opening statement was often 'Thus says the Lord'.

Their task was usually an unenviable one. Since they spoke for God, it was often necessary for them to speak out against sin, even when it was discovered in high places such as the palace or the Temple. They did not do this to be awkward or simply to be the voice of doom; their prime purpose was to bring people back to God in repentance and obedience.

The stubbornness of human nature made their task difficult and dangerous – many were martyred for their faithfulness to God and man. Jesus himself foresaw this conflict when he called Jerusalem the killer of prophets and the stoner of the messengers of God. He declared that there he, too, would be murdered.

The people of Jesus' day often recognised him as a prophet. This is all the more remarkable since it was commonly believed that the voice of prophecy had been silent for 300 years! The people felt that now, in Jesus, God was speaking to them again, performing mighty acts. On at least two occasions (in John's Gospel) people first recognised Jesus as a prophet, then as the Messiah.

This is important. Although the title 'prophet' was accurate as far as it went – Jesus himself and some of the first preachers used it, though sparingly – it is not a complete description of him. Jesus is, after all, the one about whom the Old Testament prophets spoke. He is the *subject* of their message rather than simply another messenger; he is the one who brings prophecy to its climax by being in himself its message. As God's true spokesman, Jesus has – and is – the last word.

2. God's sacrifice: Jesus the suffering servant

With this title, says Oscar Cullmann, 'we come straight to the heart of New Testament Christology.' This, says William Barclay, might well be 'the title in the light of which all the other titles of Jesus must be seen'.

This may seem a little surprising: Jesus never actually calls himself the 'servant of the Lord' and the term is only directly applied to him in one place in the Gospels. But when we look at the Old Testament background, we can see evidence of the servant idea all over the place. It was perhaps the model on which Jesus based most of what he said and did.

The title 'servant of the Lord' was given to many of the great men of the Old Testament. Abraham, Moses, King David and the prophet Elijah were all called God's servants. The title was also given to the *nation* of Israel. In four remarkable passages (sometimes called the 'Servant Songs') Isaiah, speaking in God's voice, referred to a mysterious unidentified figure as 'my servant'. This servant has a missionary task: to establish God's justice throughout the earth, to be a light for the nations and to be the instrument of their salvation. Though the servant works in a gentle and unobtrusive way, his task is extremely difficult, full of discouragements and persecution. At times it almost seems as if his work is in vain, but he sticks at it because he has great confidence that God is with him and will finally vindicate his efforts.

The final servant song (Isaiah 52:13 to 53:12) is the climax of this painful but promising process. It tells of the servant's awful disfigurement on account of what he is suffering. Those looking on – nations and kings – are appalled at what they see, but they are even more dismayed when, with growing wonder, they begin to comprehend that the servant's sufferings are not for his sins but for *theirs*! With gracious, gentle patience he bears the weight of the world's wrongdoing so that he might 'justify many' and win a great victory.

Jewish theologians grappled long and hard with these passages, trying to identify the mysterious sufferer. Theories multiplied and abounded. Was the servant the nation of Israel? Was he an individual and, if so, who? Was he a people or was he a person? As we examine the servant songs, we can see how they could fit either of these two categories or neither! Perhaps the answer lies in the way in which, in Hebrew thinking, the individual could represent the group and vice versa. The servant idea could refer to the nation and, at the same time, it could refer to an 'ideal' Israel, its true spiritual core. Indeed, it could be narrowed down even further to refer to an individual as well.

How Jesus must have seen himself reflected in these passages – especially the fourth one! It must have been as if he was gazing into a mirror. He saw there one who must tread the path of obedience in the face of the world's indifference and hostility. He saw a lonely sufferer who must bear the crushing weight of the world's sins and give his life a ransom for many.

But he also saw there the one who represents the many, the person who stands in for the people. Jesus recognised that he would fulfil the servant's role when, on the cross, he would represent every person in the world. There they and their sins would be executed and buried with him so that, as he burst up out of the grave, they too would rise with him to live a new and indestructible life.

3. God's man: Jesus the Son of Man

If 'servant' was the best description of what Jesus had come to be, then 'Son of Man' is what he mostly liked to call himself. This title is used eighty-one times in the Gospels, only by Jesus and only when referring to himself. No one else in the Gospels uses it to address him or describe him, so it was obviously Jesus' own special name for himself. It was carefully chosen to express some important aspects of what he had come into the world to be and to do.

'Son of Man' translates a phrase in Aramaic (the language Jesus spoke) and Hebrew (the language of the Old Testament) which simply means 'man' or 'human being'. By using the phrase, Jesus may have wished to emphasise his humanity, the way in which he had made himself frail and vulnerable by becoming a man. Or he may have been emphasising the fact that humankind was important enough for God to enter the human race. But since Jesus used the title when making some of his greatest claims, there is obviously more to the phrase than that.

Jesus' use of 'Son of Man' seemed to be linked with Daniel 7:3 to 14. Here, in a remarkable vision, Daniel saw someone who is described as 'one like a son of man'. Daniel saw the rise and fall of cruel and rapacious earthly empires – symbolised by fearsome beasts who rise out of the 'sea' of world history. These 'beasts' represent the successive empires of Babylonia, Assyria, Persia and the Greek Seleucid Empire. But in Daniel's vision the days of such world governments are numbered. At the height of the last empire's career, God takes power away from savage rulers and puts it into the gentle and humane hands of the Son of Man.

Who is this mysterious person? A clue can be found in Daniel 7:18, where it is said that 'the saints of the Most High' are *also* given earthly dominion. Daniel appears to be saying that Israel, so long savagely mauled by brutal earthly rulers, will itself at last come to power and reign in a godly and humane way. Once again we see, as we saw in the use of the servant title, how in Hebrew thought an individual can represent a whole group, even a whole nation. In this case it is the Son of Man who stands in for Israel and who personifies it.

Once again we see how easily and naturally Jesus was able to see himself in the role of the one who represents the many. As the Son of Man, he is the true Israel, obedient to God's commands and fulfilling his will in a way that the nation never managed to do.

Sometimes Jesus used the title 'Son of Man' as a substitute for the personal pronoun 'I'. Sometimes he used it when he was making his greatest claims and declarations. He used it when speaking about the glory that would later be his – with sayings related to his second coming and the final judgment of the world. It was a title that spoke of the majesty and power that was rightfully his and which, though hidden during his earthly life, would some day be fully revealed to all humanity.

Imagine, then, the absolute astonishment of his hearers when Jesus repeatedly used the title 'Son of Man' in connection with his sufferings and death! He did what the Jewish theologians had never done: he ran together the power and glory of the Son of Man with the sufferings and humiliations of the servant of the Lord! These two, said Jesus, are one and the same. The way that heavenly majesty was being revealed in a lost and sinful world was through humble and sacrificial service.

The Son of Man, before he could take his place on the throne, would have to go by way of the cross. Love would come down in great humility and bleed and die – and do so for all humanity – before it could be elevated again to the heavenly throne to await its victorious recognition by all creation.

4. God's companion: Jesus as Lord

'Lord' is the most commonly used title for Jesus in the New Testament. Although it occurs before his death and resurrection, it is more often used to refer to the *risen* Christ. The personal surrender of their lives to him, along with his authority (over evil spirits, individuals and crowds), convinced his disciples that he was Lord. But it was his resurrection that made the matter plain. For example, in his letters (all written about Jesus and the church *after* his resurrection), Paul uses the title more than 200 times. 'Lord' actually became a synonym for 'Jesus'.

The Greek word *kurios* has about it the air of authority. The head of a family, the director of a business, the owner of a property were all called 'lord'. Governors, military commanders and eventually Roman emperors all took the title – even the many gods of the Graeco-Roman world. One special use of *kurios* is in the Greek version of the

Old Testament, the Septuagint. It is used there to translate the sacred (Hebrew) name of God. So for any Greek-speaking Jew it would have been the normal way to address him. Naturally, when the resurrection of Jesus removed from the minds of the first Christians the last vestiges of misunderstanding about him, they suddenly realised that many of the Old Testament 'Lord' passages referred to him. Their earliest baptismal creed was quite possibly 'Jesus is Lord'.

When the first Christians said 'Jesus is Lord', they were making the highest claim they could for him. They meant that Jesus had been exalted to his Father's throne, with supreme power and authority. He was now the unseen controller of human history. Although humanity and evil spiritual forces were still openly opposed to Jesus, the whole creation was now moving towards its climax. Eventually every knee would bow to him and every tongue confess his name; his hidden lordship would be plain for all to see.

When the first Christians worshipped Jesus as Lord, they recognised him also as Lord of their own personal lives. He was master of their hopes, dreams and ambitions – of their homes, their families, jobs and possessions. There was *nothing* in life that did not come under his control. When they called him 'Lord', they were not simply remembering what he had done for them in the past; they now saw him as their representative at God's right hand. There he could have daily fellowship with them, interceding for them and bringing their prayers before his Father.

5. God's mind: Jesus as the Word

This title takes us back as far as it is possible to go: back to the beginning of all things, back into the heart and mind of God. The term 'word' (*logos*) was a popular concept in the ancient world. It meant either a thought hidden in someone's mind or that thought openly expressed. The Greeks also used the term to describe the world-soul that permeates the universe and holds it together, permeating human minds and giving them reason or wisdom. When Jews used the term 'word', they thought of it as a link between God's thoughts and intentions and this material world. When God spoke, matter was created. When he said to nothingness 'let something be', matter actually came into existence.

God is a communicator. As with us, it is through his word that God communicates. But God's word is not just a sound, a lofty idea or a principle. It is a *person*. From the beginning the Word has been God's intimate companion, so completely revealing him that the revelation was actually God himself!

To John, this must have been a staggering thought. As a first-century Jew, he would have had a very exalted view of God and his unity. But as John develops the idea in his Gospel, it all begins to make sense. God's word to us has been 'earthed' in our world. God plainly spells out just what he is like – in a human personality.

God 'spoke' the universe into being. Further, he has done so in such a way that his 'voice' – if we are willing to hear it – is still ringing out through its vast and wonderful structure. The universe's silent speech or 'sign language' tells us that all the matter we see came from God's great mind. In the beauty of our world and its complexity, his great power and wisdom – 'his everlasting power and deity' (Romans 1:20, NEB) – is able, though invisible, to be 'seen'.

God's speech or word became clearer still through the many different ministries of the long line of prophets and priests that he sent to his people in Old Testament times. The message of these spiritual teachers moved towards a climax in which a clearer and clearer picture of God emerged. His word, they began to see, would be spoken to them in some open and final form. Instead of being simply a word *about* him, it would actually be God *himself*! And so, said John (thinking of Jesus), when the time was ripe 'the Word became flesh and made his dwelling among us' (John 1:14).

In Jesus, God's Word in human flesh, God has made his final and most definitive statement about himself. He had never gone this far before and will never have to do so again. All we will ever need to know about him in this world has been said. His heart and his mind has been translated into what we know best – into the life of a human being.

We now know that the same great power which spoke the universe into being reaches out to the sick, sad and sinful and was prepared to make the supreme sacrifice for them. The mind that thought up galaxies, sending them spinning into space, which set rivers and mountains and forests in their place, is a mind of love which consented to enter deeply into what it had created – to bleed and die for it.

We have seen five of the Bible's own interpretations of Jesus. Deeply influenced by Jesus himself and assisted by his Spirit, the New Testament writers carefully explained and expounded the whole truth about him. Their inspired insights help us not only to see him as the man of Nazareth, but also as God's Son, the Lord of glory and the master of time and eternity.

8

Death and resurrection

DATES IN HISTORY ARE MILEPOSTS in a long journey. They record the rise and fall of rulers, discoveries, wars, treaties and economic agreements. They mark the passing of remarkable people and remarkable events.

Christians have always claimed that when BC gave way to AD, nothing would ever be the same again. Jesus' entry into this world would change the course of history. It would begin to move us towards a finale in which God would be all in all. It was, say Christians, that point in time when God and humanity came face-to-face with each other and where the mystery of this world and its life was revealed.

In all the years of Jesus' life, there was one event that brought all this sharply into focus: his crucifixion. In one momentous week he brought to a head all he had taught and stood for. He walked into the holy (and bloody) city of Jerusalem, a hornet's nest of hostility and suspicion, forcing a showdown with the forces of evil and with those in whom these were entrenched. He was not the helpless victim of circumstances: he was a willing volunteer.

Countdown to crucifixion

In this chapter we trace the events of that week, the way in which various personalities and influences paved the road to the cross. We will see how political, spiritual, social and religious forces combined to condemn Jesus to death.

❏ SUNDAY:

It is a familiar theme in Hollywood Westerns to see one man pitted against a whole town. Powerful and oppressive people are in control and have so browbeaten its residents that they offer no resistance. Then the hero comes! He challenges Mr Big and his friends, but no one is brave enough to offer him any support. The tempo rises until the hero, like Jesus in Jerusalem, walks down Main Street to force a showdown and outguns everybody.

One real difference between this scenario and Jesus is, of course, that Jesus had no gun (or any ancient equivalent), nor even the angelic 'deputies' that he could have called in. He did not even have a horse (a military mount for a military messiah), though his donkey was the correct mount to fulfil an ancient prophecy about the coming of Israel's true king (Zechariah 9:9).

Jesus was coming into town armed only with love, a 'weapon' which appears so weak and vulnerable, but is in fact the most powerful force on earth. He was coming as a peacemaker whose sacrifice on the cross would bring true harmony between God and all the warring elements of humankind.

❑ MONDAY:

In Westerns, the shoot-out often happens in the saloon. For Jesus, the first real confrontation was in the Temple. Here, he took on the priestly establishment, driving out those who had changed this holy sanctuary into a market place. The ecclesiastical authorities had decreed that it was appropriate to haggle for sacrificial animals or change foreign money (at a profit) into special Temple coins.

As a small boy Jesus had called the Temple his 'Father's house' (Luke 2:49). Now, with an almost proprietary air, he speaks in God's name about the way in which *his* house was being desecrated by 'thieves'. It was as if he was cleaning up the family residence, sweeping out the rubbish (and rubbish-makers) which had accumulated in its courts.

Jesus was always on the side of ordinary people, always grieved when he saw anything that hindered them in their search for God. He was angered by the cheats and swindlers who were making it even harder for them to fulfil their religious duties. Jesus was especially furious to think that, when foreign pilgrims came to the Court of the Gentiles, turning wistfully from their paganism in the hope that they might hear some echo of God in the Temple, they were instead confronted with a rabble of noisy money-grubbers.

Nothing that Jesus could have done would have angered his opponents more than the cleansing of the Temple. He had taken them on in their own territory and challenged them to do their worst.

❑ TUESDAY:

The battle on Tuesday was a war of words. At least four deputations came to Jesus to engage him in controversy, hoping to trip him up on what he said. They wanted to know by what authority he acted as he did. They tried to get him to make politically dangerous statements about paying tribute to the Romans. The sceptical Sadducees posed some curly questions about life after death; and the legalistic Pharisees, not to be outdone, tried to get Jesus to pontificate on what was the most important commandment. His answers to all these questions staggered his opponents. They were 'astonished', 'amazed' and eventually silenced.

Jesus counterattacked with a series of parables. The most telling one was about an absentee landlord who had equipped a vineyard, letting it out to tenant farmers who could pay their rent in either money or produce (described in chapter 3).

One did not need to be an intellectual giant to see what Jesus was driving at, especially when one remembered that the 'vineyard' was a well-known symbol for the nation of Israel. The 'owner' was God, the 'tenants' the current rulers and leaders of Israel. The 'messengers' were, of course, the long line of prophets whom God had sent to his people and who had so often been rejected and ill-treated. Jesus was the 'son'.

By making a distinction between himself and the prophets, he was publicly claiming a unique relationship with God. He was God's only Son, his last word to Israel, their final chance before they shut themselves out of God's purposes for the world. No wonder their reaction was 'may this never be'. No wonder they immediately began to look for a way to arrest him – and so, in fact, fulfil the parable!

❑ WEDNESDAY:

Ordinary people are not usually remembered for long after they die. Not being celebrities, they usually simply sink into obscurity. But now and again one or other of them as if almost by accident stumbles onto the pages of the history books. By being at the right time at the right place, they get caught up in events bigger than themselves.

One such person was an obscure woman who came in off the street while Jesus was at dinner. She carried with her what was no doubt the most valuable thing she possessed, an alabaster jar filled with a perfume as expensive as any top quality perfume today. In an extravagant act of love, she broke the jar and anointed Jesus' head with its contents. Jesus recognised the beauty of her sacrifice, despite the shocked and disparaging remarks made by others. She had, he said, used the last available opportunity to anoint him for burial. As the fragrance of the broken phial filled the room, so, said Jesus, the memory of what she had done would permeate the whole world.

Today her loving gesture is better known than most actions in history: it is enshrined in the pages of the world's best-seller and has been translated into hundreds of languages. The fragrance of her love indeed still fills the earth.

☐ THURSDAY:

With the awful events of the next day now weighing heavily upon him, it was time for Jesus to bid his disciples goodbye. It was time for a farewell supper. But the way in which Jesus conducted the meal was to make the word 'farewell' almost inappropriate. He was, after all, not going to 'leave' them at all: he was simply exchanging a physical presence for a spiritual one. In his risen life and through the gift of his 'other self' (the Holy Spirit), he would continue to be with them in an even more intimate way.

Whenever they broke bread and drank wine together in remembrance of him, he would be present with them. When they re-enacted those symbolic acts, it would always make his impending sacrifice on the cross more vivid for them.

Jesus employed dramatic action language, as the prophets had done, to show what he would do for us: his body would be broken like the bread, his blood poured out like the wine. But he also showed what kind of response we should make to his dying love.

Just as we take the bread and wine into our bodies so that they become part of our physical bloodstream, so by faith we may reach out and take to ourselves the spiritual benefits of Christ's death on the cross. His 'farewell' supper has become for us (as it was for the first Christians and every generation between their time and ours) a constant reminder that Jesus has never said 'goodbye' to his church and never will till the end of time.

Death and resurrection

After such a dramatic reminder of what awaited him, Jesus now sought for a secluded place where he could finally come to terms with the physical, mental and spiritual battle ahead of him. He went to Gethsemane, a favourite place of seclusion at the foot of the Mount of Olives. Here the full force of what he was about to experience overwhelmed him.

It was not merely physical death or suffering that daunted him, of course. It was the nightmare vision of all the sins of humanity laid upon his sinless shoulders. The horror and abandonment of it all momentarily blotted out the light and Jesus cried out for a reprieve. To be mocked by cruel men, pierced by nails and tortured by thirst was terrible enough. But to lose sight of his Father's face as the dark cloud of sin and guilt rolled over him was more than he could bear.

As the hours dragged by and as his 'supporters' drifted into sleep, Jesus wrestled on until he had finally won through. It was the *acceptance* of God's will that carried the day: 'Father, the hour has come. Give glory to your Son, so that the Son may give glory to you.' This had always been the compass point by which he steered. With complete confidence in his Father's loving purposes, Jesus would hold his course to the bitter end.

With the battle over and a cry of warning to the sleeping disciples, the quiet of the garden was suddenly broken by the clank of swords and the shouts of armed men. The traitor approached and, with a tender kiss, sent Jesus on his way to the cross.

Death and resurrection

❏ FRIDAY:
Fair-minded people have always seen the crucifixion of Jesus as an act of gross injustice. To execute the best man who ever lived simply for being what he was has always seemed to thoughtful people to be evidence of a fatal moral flaw in human nature.

It is easy enough to lay the sole blame at the feet of the cynical religious leaders or the careless Roman administrators. But the fact is that these people were *our* representatives, the ones who happened to be on the spot at the time – who did to Jesus what we have all done to him in our own way and in our own culture.

As the negro spiritual puts it:

Were you there when they crucified my Lord?
Were you there when they crucified my Lord?
O, sometimes it causes me to tremble, tremble, tremble.
Were you there when they crucified my Lord?

In keeping with the injustice of the crucifixion, Jesus was hustled towards the cross with indecent haste, many legal rules designed to safeguard the innocent swept aside. Jesus was to be tried before a kangaroo court in the early hours of Friday.

The trial of Jesus
The Jewish part of the trial concentrated on religious matters. After unsuccessful attempts to pin various charges on Jesus the high priest, Caiaphas, came right to the point. Was he or was

he not the Messiah, the Son of God? Jesus replied, 'You will see the Son of Man sitting at the right hand of the Mighty One and coming on the clouds of heaven' (Mark 14:6). Triumphantly Caiaphas now rested his case, confident that the Sanhedrin would judge Jesus' words as a supreme act of blasphemy and condemn him to death.

The Roman part of the trial was necessary because at this time in history the Romans had taken from the Jews the power to condemn people to death. But of what use would a religious charge be? To get the Romans to act, it was necessary to prove that Jesus was a political offender, a danger to the Roman administration. So when Jesus was taken to Pontius Pilate, the Roman governor, he was charged with subverting the nation, forbidding the payment of taxes and claiming to be a king. Pilate was obviously not convinced by these charges but, because of his various political blunders, he knew that he could not summarily dismiss them. Jesus' accusers also knew this very well.

Pilate clearly stood in awe of Jesus and made desperate attempts to get him off the hook. He sent him to Herod (hearing that he was a 'Galilean'); he had him scourged with whips (as substitute punishment); he offered to release him instead of a well-known local criminal. But it was all to no avail. The religious leaders had Pilate over a political barrel. When they resorted to cries of 'if you let this man go you are no friend of Caesar', he capitulated and, against his better judgment, sent Jesus to the cross.

The crucifixion of Jesus

Who could ever have guessed that when God was to take us into his deepest confidence, we would find ourselves in front of a hideous instrument of torture: a cross? Who would ever have imagined that the very essence of God's nature, love, would be translated into human experience as blood, sweat and agony? But, say the Bible writers, this is exactly what has happened. They describe the crucifixion in stark but not in gruesome terms. They do not give sensational details or try to play on our emotions and yet, as the story unfolds, it is moving and poignant. We are conscious that we are standing on holy, though bloodstained ground.

For Jesus, the whole day had of course been an exceedingly harrowing one. From before dawn he had been grilled by questioners, unjustly accused, deserted by friends and roughed up by soldiers. Now he must endure the cross itself, a fate reserved by the Romans for slaves or for the worst sort of criminals and seen by Jews as evidence that the victim had a curse laid upon him (Deuteronomy 21:23).

The description of Jesus' ordeal is filled with words and incidents of great meaning. Some of the words were uttered with malicious intent, but the cross, God's strange place of revelation, transformed them into the truth. For example, over Jesus' head was his 'accusation' in three languages: 'This is Jesus, King of the Jews.' This was Pilate's sarcastic jibe at his tormentors, a kind of nervous joke, but the cross gave new weight to his careless words. A crown of thorns was jammed down on

Jesus' brow. The King of Love suffered for our sins so that the evil empire of Satan could be overthrown and God's true kingdom set up in human hearts.

Last words

Those who hounded Jesus to the cross taunted him still. They said of him, 'he saved others, but he cannot save himself'. Once again, the cross transformed their bitter words: to save us he *had* to lose his own life.

Jesus' own words from the cross are significant. He prayed that his executioners be forgiven; he hands his mother over to the care of his friend; he welcomes a repentant fellow-sufferer into paradise. But perhaps no words are more fraught with meaning than the awful cry that comes at three o'clock in the afternoon as darkness prematurely falls: 'My God, my God, why have you forsaken me?' Jesus was plumbing the murky depths of the universe, crushed by the unspeakable weight of our sins, unable any more to see the face of his Father. It is a moment of unfathomable mystery, at the centre of what he had come into the world to do.

Unexpected turnaround

Jesus, say the creeds, was 'crucified, dead and buried'. And so, too, were the hopes and dreams of his followers. When they sadly trudged away from his tomb, they mentally said goodbye forever to his great vision of the coming kingdom. But Jesus, who had astonished them so often, was to do so again, this time almost beyond their wildest dreams. Within a few days they were convinced that he had risen from the dead! This was not a pious belief that grew up later within the church, but the belief out of which the church itself grew. The church, Christianity itself, is undoubtedly a post-resurrection phenomenon.

The conviction that Jesus was alive rested on two facts: first, his tomb was found to be empty; second, a considerable number of his disciples met and talked with him. If this belief had not become absolutely central to their thinking, the Jesus movement would no doubt have simply faded away.

Alternative explanations

The critics of Christianity have often made strenuous attempts to debunk the resurrection. They have suggested, for example, that Jesus fainted on the cross and revived later in the cool of the tomb. They have suggested the disciples mistook their way and came to an already vacant gravesite. Or else friends (or enemies) of Jesus stole the body to bolster (or undermine) the resurrection belief. However, none of these theories appears to fit the circumstances.

Would expert Roman executioners have assumed him dead if he were not so? Could a badly wounded man revive in the bitter chill of a Jerusalem Easter, unwrap his burial bandages, remove a heavy stone and then, after walking for miles on badly injured feet, inspire his frightened followers to believe in his conquest of death?

Would the highly ethical Jesus that we read of in the Gospels have been prepared to deceive people in this way? And if his followers had stolen his body, would they have built their faith on a lie – even die for it? If his enemies had stolen the body, then to produce it would have been the trump card that would have demolished the Christian claim.

In modern times, the objection which appeals to many people is that the so-called appearances of Jesus were hallucinations. But once again the objection does not fit the facts. Hallucinations tend to conform to certain rules; for example, hallucinations occur among people of an identifiable psychological type and are highly individualistic. In the Gospels, a recognisable Jesus was seen by many different types and temperaments – on at least one occasion, by about 500 people at the same time.

Those who saw him in this way were completely transformed. The cowardly Peter became a bold preacher; Jesus' sceptical brother, James, became a very influential church leader; later on, the persecuting Saul of Tarsus became the greatest Christian missionary of all time.

Faith ignited, reason repaired

Of course, those who approach the Jesus story absolutely convinced that a resurrection could not occur will not be convinced by *any* evidence. They will have decided the issue before examining it and they will see it all as a put-up job. For his part God, like the Jesus of the Gospels, will never compel anyone to believe. He gives enough evidence for us to be able to accept it with intellectual integrity, but then we must go beyond – though not against – reason.

We must accept the fact that our own thinking processes are impaired by our egocentric refusal to let God reign in our lives. We must allow his Spirit to build on our partial grasp of the truth, to enlarge our vision and heal our reason. In other words, we must receive from God the gift of faith which, because it is not based on wishful thinking but on the kind of evidence that we have in the Gospels, is actually the beginning of real repair in our thought processes.

With an open mind and open heart, we can look into the Gospels and see Jesus risen from the dead and alive forevermore. We see him set free from time and space so that he may make himself known to us. And he does – when in genuine humility we reach out to him.

God, the ever-waiting Father, stands ready to welcome us. He longs more than anything else that we should come to know him personally. This is God's plan for us – and for all people everywhere.

Discussion questions

Discussion questions

Finding the real Jesus

1. What do the people *you* meet say about Jesus? What is your response to what they say?

2. How would you answer someone who said that Jesus was:
(a) 'just a man' – a great, good, inspired man, but by no means divine?
(b) a political liberator, come to rescue the poor and the oppressed?
(c) a mysterious person not really understood by anyone?

3. What would you expect to see in the life of a person without sin? Since it is generally accepted that those closest to God are most conscious of their sins, what does John 8:46 tell us about Jesus' conscience? How does such a claim fit in with his general character?

4. What do the following verses tell us about Jesus as a teacher?
Matthew 7:24, 26, 28 and 29; Matthew 11:29; Luke 20:39; Luke 11:52; Luke 19:47 and 48; John 3:2; John 7:46.

5. What would you say to someone who said, 'I can accept the fact that Jesus was a great man and a great teacher, but I cannot accept his great claims for himself or that he could perform miracles'?

History in the making

1. From reading Luke 1:1 to 4, what do you think were the author's methods, aims and objectives? Comparing this with John's approach (John 21:24 and 25), can you see how this might resemble or differ from the aims of a modern historian?

2. In what way might your attitude to the Gospels affect what you see in them?

3. Jewish, Roman and Greek influences were a positive preparation for Jesus' coming into the ancient world. What influences today might prepare people to listen to what Jesus had to say?

4. The uncertainties of life and a spiritual vacuum in the wider society were the negative influences which helped people take Jesus seriously during the first century. Are there similar influences at work today? What are they?

5. When Paul wrote to the Galatian Christians he said, 'Before your very eyes Jesus Christ was clearly portrayed as crucified' (Galatians 3:1). Since Jesus had died some years before, in what way could the Galatians 'see' him on the cross? In what way can we – twenty centuries later – see him? In what way does his history blend with ours?

Discussion questions

The Jesus story

1. Read Matthew 4:1 to 11. Jesus' temptations were, in one sense, uniquely his own. But since he lived and died for all people, they also apply to us. In what way:
(a) are we similarly tempted?
(b) can we apply the scriptures Jesus quoted to our temptations?

2. In Jesus' 'year of popularity' he taught and he performed miracles, especially of healing. These two aspects of his ministry were blended together. Read Mark 2:1 to 12. In the event recorded, how does Jesus teach through healing? What does he teach?

3. At the height of his popularity, Jesus fed a great crowd of people. As usual he was trying to teach them something and, as usual, they missed the point. What was Jesus trying to get them to see (see John 6:25ff)? What was the crowd so intent on finding that it prevented them from understanding Jesus' message?

4. When the apostles – with Peter as spokesman – openly acknowledged Jesus' true identity (Mark 8:27 to 30), Jesus began to speak about his coming crucifixion. Peter, as spokesman again, protested, receiving a stinging rebuke from Jesus (Mark 8:31 to 33). Why was Jesus so tough on him? Why did he call him 'Satan'? What did he mean by 'Your thoughts don't come from God but from man'?

5. Jesus was no stranger to controversy. A typical dialogue that he had with the religious leaders in Jerusalem was in regard to the authority with which he taught. Read Matthew 21:23 to 27. What was Jesus trying to get them to see?

Discussion questions

The kingdom of God

1. What do you think Jesus meant by the phrase 'the kingdom of God'? How would you explain it to someone who had never heard of it before?

2. What kind of leader were the people of Jesus' day looking for? In what way did this differ from Jesus' concept of the kingdom and its king?

3. Jesus plainly shared the 'secrets' of the kingdom with his disciples. But with the crowds he explained what the kingdom was like in a series of parables. What clues to its nature do you find in the following parables in Matthew chapter 13?
- The parable of the sower (verses 1 to 9, 18 to 23)
- The parable of the weeds (verses 24 to 30, 36 to 43)
- The parable of the mustard seed and the yeast (verses 31 to 33)
- The parables of the hidden treasure and the pearl (verses 44 to 46)
- The parable of the net (verses 47 to 50)

4. Entry into the kingdom is by God's generous invitation and is freely offered to all, regardless of how they have lived. But the lifestyle of the kingdom is morally well above average. How do you reconcile these two factors?

Discussion questions

5. What are the main hindrances to people entering God's kingdom today:
- ❑ Reluctance to change?
- ❑ Money and pleasure-seeking?
- ❑ Indecisiveness?
- ❑ Other things?

Life in the kingdom

1. To love God with all of our being and to love our neighbours as much as we love ourselves is a simple, direct and very challenging obligation. How would you apply it to the following issues:
- Choosing an occupation
- The use of time
- Economic matters, especially the pursuit of money for its own sake
- Sexuality inside of marriage
- Sexuality outside of marriage

2. In the Sermon on the Mount, Jesus taught that life in the kingdom was a 'like father, like son' affair. Read Matthew 5:43 to 48. How do you think this could be applied practically in your work, community or home situation? How could it be applied to those who try to make life difficult for you?

3. How is Jesus' command to love God and love others related to God's law? In attempting to obey God and live by his standards, how can we avoid becoming legalistic?

Discussion questions

4. Since Jesus put such a strong emphasis on the motives and intentions of the heart, do you think it is possible to do the right thing for the wrong reasons? If you felt that you were doing this, do you think you should give up doing the 'right' thing or try to get a new motivation? How would you go about getting it?

5. Love's standards are simple but very high and we often fall short of them or rebel against them. At such times, what part do you think God's own love and forgiveness plays in changing our attitudes and setting us on the path of obedience again?

Claims and miracles

1. What would you say to someone who said that he or she accepted Jesus as a wonderful person and a great teacher, but did not believe that he was the Son of God or that he performed miracles?

2. Why did Jesus often make indirect claims for himself? Why did he not use his remarkable powers to *compel* people to accept him for what he was? How does that relate to his approach to people today?

3. Some people say that miracles just do not happen. How would you answer this statement?

4. Jesus obviously did not use miracles as 'tricks' to impress people and he sometimes refused to perform them when people demanded them for the wrong reasons. How *did* Jesus use miracles?

5. Some Christians today think that a re-emergence of miracles would have a great impact on unbelievers. Other Christians do not agree and maintain that Jesus' and the apostles' miracles were unique, an endorsement of the fact that God was making once-for-all revelations of himself to humankind. What do you think?

Discussion questions

The titles of Jesus

1. The Samaritan woman mentioned in John 4:4 to 42 came to believe that Jesus was a prophet. Why did she come to this conclusion? What led her to see even more in him than that?

2. Read Isaiah 52:13 to 53:12. Write down what you think Jesus must have seen of himself in this passage. What would he have seen in the passage to indicate the involvement of others beside himself?

3. When Jesus used the term 'Son of Man' to describe himself, he often did so in connection with the glory that would one day be his (see, for example, Matthew 19:28; Luke 17:26 and 30). But Jesus also used the term to speak of his sufferings and death (see Mark 9:31; Matthew 26:2). How can these two types of statements be reconciled?

4. 'Jesus is Lord' may have been the earliest Christian creed. How would you translate it into modern terms? What would it mean as applied to our work, our homes and families, our possessions, our ambitions and our personal plans?

5. Jesus is called 'the Word' (John 1:1). What does this title tell us about God's communication with us?

Discussion questions

Death and resurrection

1. Why do you think Jesus went first to the Temple in his confrontation with the powers-that-be in Jerusalem?

2. Tuesday's controversies were particularly applicable to the times. Do you think Jesus would take up the same issues with modern people? If not, what sort of thing would he concentrate on today?

3. What was it that Jesus mostly shrank from as he prayed in the garden? What was it that kept him committed to his awful destiny?

4. 'Were you there when they crucified my Lord' says the old Negro spiritual. In what way do you think that you were 'there'?

5. What evidences for the resurrection do you find most convincing? How would you defend the teaching of Christ's physical resurrection to someone sceptical of it? If you are in a group discussion, some role-play might be stimulating.